# Parents' and Carers' Guide
## for Able and Talented Children

## Barry Teare

Published by Network Educational Press Ltd
PO Box 635
Stafford
ST16 1BF

First published 2004
© Barry Teare 2004

ISBN 1 85539 128 7

Edited by Dawn Booth
Design, layout, illustrations and cover by Kerry Ingham

Printed in Great Britain by MPG Books Ltd, Bodmin, Cornwall

## ACKNOWLEDGEMENTS

Many thanks to the 'team' at Network Educational Press for their encouragement, skills, support and hard work – Jane Phillips, Dawn Booth, Kerry Ingham and Neil Hawkins. The author is indebted to Stella Cutland and Phil Creek for their comments on the 'raw material'. A special thank you to Christina Teare for her encouragement and support generally and for her suggestions and comments.

At the time of going to press all addresses and contact details are correct; however they may change at short notice, especially email and website addresses.

# CONTENTS

# INTRODUCTION

## AIMS OF THE BOOK

- To inform parents and carers on the current thinking about able and talented pupils, including a brief description of the major government initiatives.
- To assist parents and carers in understanding the needs of their able children.
- To explain to parents and carers, in ordinary terms, the principles behind good provision for able and talented children.
- To inform parents and carers in order that they may carry out a meaningful dialogue with the schools attended by their able and talented children.
- To help parents and carers decide how best to support their able and talented children.
- To provide information on where to obtain additional help and advice, and what activities are available.
- To provide a wealth of practical activities under separate subject headings.
- To advise on what is suitable reading for able and talented children.

## Symbols used in this book

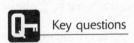 Key questions

 Important messages

 Action points

# SECTION 1
## ISSUES

## WHAT'S IN A NAME?

> *'What's in a name? that which we call a rose*
> *By any other name would smell as sweet'*

William Shakespeare, *Romeo and Juliet*

Many definitions have been used to describe the children at the heart of this book:

- able
- clever
- gifted and talented
- talented
- able and talented
- exceptionally able
- more able
- very able
- abler
- gifted
- most able.

The government has adopted the term 'gifted and talented', so that is the term that you will find used in most schools. In schools within the Excellence in Cities initiative, two-thirds of the 'gifted and talented' may be gifted in one or more subjects (other than art, music or PE) and one-third are identified as talented in the creative arts, music or PE and sport.

Some people are unhappy with the inclusion of the word 'gifted' for two reasons:

1. The term appears very exclusive.
2. It suggests that only a few exceptional people, such as the likes of a Mozart or an Einstein, are included in the group.

Many practitioners, including the author of this book, prefer the more general name 'able and talented', which is the phrase used in the book.

Be aware that 'gifted and talented' is the official term but be prepared to meet many other descriptions. Rather like Shakespeare's rose, what we call these children is far less important than what we do to improve their education.

# THE PRESENT STATE OF PLAY

In recent years, provision for able and talented children has become an educational priority. Far from being the Cinderella area that was once the case, issues about able and talented pupils have gone to the top of the ladder.

How is your child affected by the recent developments?

The answer, to some extent, depends upon where you live.

## Excellence in Cities

This programme, containing a number of proposals for gifted and talented children, was announced by the government in March 1999. Six areas of England were initially involved: Manchester and Salford, Birmingham, a number of London Boroughs, Sheffield and Rotherham, Leeds and Bradford, and Liverpool and Knowsley. Work started in September 1999 and has since spread to a large number of other areas, including Stoke, Hull, Stockton-on-Tees and Nottingham.

The initiative began in secondary schools but later was extended to primary schools.

If your child goes to school in an Excellence in Cities area (you can check on this by enquiring at the school or at the Education Office for your area), money has been provided by the government for the following:

- Appointing people especially to promote the interests of able and talented children. They work at three levels: a 'strand' co-ordinator who is a full-time organizer for the local education authority, a 'cluster' co-ordinator who has a time allocation available to organize developments across a group of five or six neighbouring schools, a school co-ordinator who teaches for most of the week but has some time allowed to help make good provision for able and talented children in his or her own school.

- Training on the issues involving able and talented children. There is an extensive training programme for co-ordinators and money available for the shorter training of all staff. This is needed because, perhaps amazingly, most teachers still do not receive specific help on able and talented pupils in their initial teacher training. This is particularly surprising as the Teacher Training Agency requires newly qualified teachers to be able to identify able pupils and provide challenging lessons for them.

- Resources and materials that encourage thinking skills which challenge able children.

- Enrichment activities of various lengths in addition to normal lessons. These activities can be limited to a single school or they can involve pupils from a group of schools.

## Excellence in Cities clusters

Some areas have received limited funding for the purposes described above, so, as the money is given on a smaller scale, what can be organized is more modest.

## Education Action Zones

Particularly in city areas, Education Action Zones (EAZs), as they are known, have been established to drive-up standards. Provision for able and talented children is often one of the issues to receive attention. Some EAZs are soon to change their names to clusters.

## All areas

Many local education authorities (LEAs) do not receive additional funding aimed at able and talented pupils but, even so, a number make very limited amounts available out of their existing funding. This makes possible some training for teachers and enrichment courses for children but, clearly, on a more limited scale. No matter where a school is situated, there are government expectations and requirements:

- Ofsted inspects schools on a regular basis. The instructions for inspection teams were amended in January 2000 to put greater emphasis upon the needs of able and talented pupils. Both for primary and secondary schools, the Ofsted team was asked to explore:

  - *how the school identifies its gifted and talented pupils;*
  - *the awareness of staff of these pupils;*
  - *the willingness of teachers to adapt and adjust to take account of pupils' rapid development;*
  - *the school's strategies for ensuring that all teachers are able to share in providing the level of subject support needed;*
  - *how the school draws on sources of support for gifted and talented pupils.*

The Ofsted handbooks were amended again in autumn 2003. Stress is now placed upon engaging and challenging pupils – expecting the most from them. Inspectors are asked to:

> *'Observe what is done to challenge the most able pupils in the class, including those who may be identified by the school as gifted and talented. Watch for those pupils who clearly are not being challenged enough. What is the effect of lack of challenge on them? Where no obvious special provision is being made, find out why.'*

Not dealing well with able children can result in an adverse Ofsted inspection report. Schools requiring special measures have weaknesses such as 'significant underachievement by a large proportion of pupils or particular groups of pupils'. Schools with serious weaknesses may be described as such because of 'underachievement among particular groups of pupils'. Triggers that might suggest a school is underachieving include 'lack of challenge and slow progress for particular groups of pupils (for example the most able)'.

In future, all inspectors will need to address issues relating to able and talented pupils.

In other words, there are clear requirements placed on all schools, irrespective of whether or not they receive additional monies for able pupils.

- All LEAs were asked to include able pupils in their Education Action Plans; most have advisers who have the responsibility of provision for able pupils. Some run their own enrichment courses.

- All LEAs can bid for money to run summer schools for able pupils.

- Children, aged 11–16, from all areas, can apply to take part in the evening, weekend and holiday events, including summer schools, that are held locally and nationally by the National Academy for Gifted and Talented Youth at the University of Warwick, once they have been accepted as a member through their school. Opportunities for primary-age children are to be added.

 Find out whether your child's school is part of the Excellence in Cities scheme or any other similar initiative. Whatever the outcome, be aware of what the expectations on able and talented pupils are for all schools.

# WHAT CAN BE EXPECTED FROM SCHOOLS IN RELATION TO ABLE AND TALENTED CHILDREN

Schools all vary and funding for able and talented child initiatives is very different from area to area. However, all schools have been asked to move forward in making better provision available. There are a growing number of schools that are making better provision for able children.

The situation is improving, but it is still far from perfect. The following features can be expected:

- ☑ A whole-school policy document or guidelines explaining what the school is doing and intends to do.

- ☑ Policy statements on English, mathematics and other subjects, containing more specific information.

- ☑ A co-ordinator to lead the work. This person might be called the gifted and talented co-ordinator or the able child co-ordinator (ABCO). In some schools the special needs co-ordinator (SENCO) also looks after the interests of able pupils.

- ☑ General staff awareness as a result of in-service training.

- ☑ An identification system using a number of methods. This may involve the production of an able and talented register, just as there is one, compulsorily by law, for special needs children.

- ☑ Lessons and homework that take account of the particular needs of able pupils.

- ☑ A determined drive by all the staff to create a school ethos in which it is 'cool' to succeed.

- ☑ Special enrichment sessions to make additional provision across a range of subjects. These may be limited to the one school or they may involve children from neighbouring schools.

- ☑ Links with outside providers so that all talents can be followed up even if there is no internal staff expertise available.

*'A fair share of the cake.'* At one time there were many people who held the view that 'clever children can look after themselves'. Others felt that able children had been born lucky and, therefore, resources, especially at times of shortage, should be directed at those with learning problems. This is an unacceptable philosophy. All children should be given the correct provision, including the able and talented. Parents and carers should not expect more than for others, but nor should they accept less than others. Certainly in comprehensive schools (and primary schools are comprehensive in nature) there can be only one way of thinking – that all children deserve appropriate provision. Able children should not be left to their own devices, but encouraged to reach their potential. They need a fair share of the teacher's time but of an appropriate nature.

Find out what your child's school has done, and is planning to do in the future, to improve provision for able and talented pupils.

# Two-way Communication

A partnership between home and school is important for all children, including able and talented children. Two-way communication is a vital component in a successful partnership.

## From the school

How can parents and carers receive information about their able and talented children and what the school is trying to achieve?

o The school brochure is a general guide to the school's aims, ethos and opportunities. Able and talented children should be included but the information is likely to be short. However, you will get a flavour of their overall approach.

- The whole-school policy on able pupils is likely to give details about a whole range of issues – the target group, identification strategies, classroom methods, the school ethos, pastoral care, monitoring and evaluation, staff training and links with parents.

- Some schools hold a special meeting for parents and carers on the issues concerning able pupils.

- A few schools issue a small booklet for parents and carers entitled 'Helping Your Able Child'.

- When your child joins the school there will be an induction evening for new parents and carers. A variety of topics are covered including, hopefully, able and talented children.

- More individual information about your able child will be conveyed via end-of-term and end-of-year reports, parents' and carers' evenings, telephone calls and specific messages. It is sensible for the school to inform you about a change of direction for your child's education. For instance, a plan to increase the challenge and difficulty in the work, because your child is finding the normal work too easy, is something that you need to know as you may start worrying if marks go down even though the child is doing well.

There are many routes to obtaining information from the school on able and talented pupils generally and about your child specifically.

Now for the 'other side of the coin'.

## From the parents and carers

Again, there are various ways in which you can convey information and also your feelings to the school.

- When your child joins a school there are normally opportunities to make the school aware of any particular abilities and talents that he or she possesses. This can work well at that time but the situation may change later on as new abilities become apparent. Other forms of communication then need to be pursued.

- Reports often have a comment slip so that you can make remarks about your child's progress. If there does not seem to be sufficient challenge here is an opportunity to express that concern.

- Parents' and carers' evenings give you a face-to-face opportunity to discuss any problems or worries. You can also ask about future plans and what the school will be offering.

- During the periods between formal communication, a telephone call or a letter can be used. You may wish to address this to the class teacher, the head of year (in a secondary school) or the co-ordinator for able and talented children. A meeting will probably follow such a call or letter.

- Some schools involve parents and carers in their identification system. This is known as parental/carer nomination or parental/carer referral. If so, you would be asked to write about any subjects or activities in which your child is particularly able, either in school or outside. Such a response would likely require you to give your reasons for your nomination. The things you say might just confirm what the school already knows but that too is helpful. Sometimes you may have points to add that have not yet been picked up by the school. After all, you see your able child in very different circumstances than the school and for more time. It is not surprising, therefore, that you may have something valuable to add to the school's information.

 Make sure that the school has all the available information about the special abilities and talents of your child. Misunderstandings are more likely when there is no proper two-way communication. As a result, provision for your child might be impaired and less effective.

# How the school might identify your child as able and talented

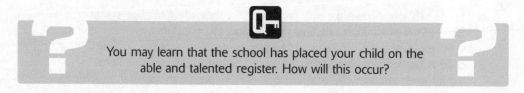

You may learn that the school has placed your child on the able and talented register. How will this occur?

Some methods will almost certainly have been used, others may have been used.

## The big two

### Test scores and statistical data

No identification scheme can operate without reference to test scores and results. A child doing much better than average in SATs, reading tests, public examinations or specific tests like CATs (cognitive abilities tests), will be regarded as able because he or she is performing better than the majority of other children. Used positively, tests give important information.

However, there are weaknesses and limitations in the testing systems that need to be taken into account.

- A test on a particular day might be affected by the child's health and well-being on that occasion.
- Some children do not respond very well to the test situation.
- Tests are limited in what they signify. They are designed to measure a particular ability and they should not be applied too generally.
- Some abilities and talents are not easily measured. Mathematics tests abound that produce a particular score, but it is not so easy to measure leadership ability and negotiating skills which are very important in the world of work and beyond.

o Marking schemes are often too narrow and rigid. Credit is given for the obvious answer only. An able child can give a more perceptive answer but get no credit for it because the response is not the one suggested in the marking scheme. A good example is classification, where children are asked to nominate the odd one out from a list of items. Able children see more sophisticated connections than their peers and therefore give an answer that is not the obvious one but that is still very appropriate. Here, one has the ridiculous situation that a standard response receives a mark, but a more sophisticated answer does not score because the examiner does not know what connection the child has seen, as the response is just by underlining or circling the odd one out.

o There are particular difficulties in assessing the potential ability of children for whom English is not their first language. Refugee children, for instance, would not score well on language-based tests until they had had time to improve their English.

## Teacher referral

The other method that is used universally is that of referral or nomination by the teacher who will have a wealth of evidence to draw upon – classwork, homework, oral contributions, special projects, observations of personality, character and dealings with other people. It may be that a particular spark is shown in one piece of work. Able pupils tend to send 'signals' by tackling a task in an unusual way. The child might be very obviously ahead of the rest of the class. Oral work might demonstrate much better-than-average presentational skills. The child might be a 'born leader'.

Hopefully, teacher referral places great emphasis upon the child's performance in higher-order thinking skills rather than on just superficial qualities, such as neatness and length of work. Provision is very important; how do you know what someone is capable of doing unless there is an opportunity to demonstrate it.

ALSO BE AWARE THAT THERE ARE A NUMBER OF OTHER IDENTIFICATION STRATEGIES THAT THE SCHOOL MIGHT USE.

## Outside referral

Information from outside the school is taken into account – previous schools, activities attended such as Guides and Scouts – that gives evidence of a particular ability or talent.

## Self-nomination

Your child might be asked what he or she believes is his or her particular ability or talent. This allows the child's view to be set against what everybody else is saying.

## Peer nomination

Other children are asked who they think have particular ability or talent. The question is unlikely to be asked directly but could be part of a more general questionnaire. Children have a different perspective and they see their peers in other situations.

## General checklists

Here, a number of characteristics that apply to many able children are listed. Teachers using the checklist do not look for a total match but rather that a fair number of points fit the child.

 Have a look at the list below. These are the type of points that go on to a general checklist.

1. Takes the lead in a group situation.
2. Has an 'oddball' sense of humour that delights in the absurd and may lead to being misunderstood.
3. Becomes restless quickly when bored with work because it is repetitive.
4. Can concentrate for a considerable time once really interested.
5. At least part of the time, prefers the company of adults to other children.
6. Follows a hobby or interest to almost obsessive lengths.
7. Does not respect people just because of their position – respect has to be earned.
8. Looks at situations rather differently from many peers.
9. Challenges teachers and others when not in agreement with them.
10. Takes a strong interest in areas of philosophical interest, fairness, and questions about life and death.
11. Frequently asks unusual, perceptive questions.
12. Does not go for the obvious answer.
13. Tends to prefer word humour to 'slapstick' humour.
14. Copes well with abstract work and therefore enjoys challenges, such as codes.
15. Uses specific examples to formulate general principles and rules.
16. Displays a greater understanding orally than might be assumed from the written work because of reluctance to write everything down.
17. Can be careless with simple tasks as due attention is not given.
18. Understands where a story is leading to well ahead of others.
19. Can make predictions based upon existing knowledge.
20. Chooses a complex problem to solve in preference to tasks that lack challenge.

When looking at a general checklist, not all the pointers will apply to a particular able child. You are looking for a match in many of the areas.

## Subject checklists

These are similar to the general checklist but the characteristics are confined to a particular subject, such as science, history, English or art. They are helpful in disposing of misconceptions or narrow viewpoints. Mathematics provides a really good example. Children are often placed in the top group at primary school mainly on their ability to calculate and carry out computation. This is a very misleading view: many able mathematicians have not been very accurate in calculation. The great French mathematician, Poincaré, admitted that he could not add up without making an error. Professor Ian Stewart, one of our greatest living mathematicians, expresses the view in his chapter within Melvyn Bragg's book *On Giant's Shoulders* that many of the great mathematicians had to have somebody to check their figures as it was not their strength.

Understanding what it is to be able in a particular subject is not quite as simple as might be thought.

On a checklist for mathematics the following could be included:

1. The ability to transfer what has been learned in one situation into another.
2. Deal well with abstract work; for instance, as shown in algebra.
3. Formulate general rules from specific examples.
4. Use mathematical symbols confidently.
5. Work well with data; discard irrelevant information.
6. Strength in logical reasoning.
7. Flexible, using different methods to solve a problem.
8. Seeing patterns.
9. Make appropriate predictions and hypotheses.
10. Are able to reverse a process.
11. Having learned a small number of situations, can manipulate hundreds of other examples from them.
12. Display mental agility.
13. Can visualize shapes and movement easily in, for instance, tessellations, rotations, reflections, deciding whether pentominoes are different shapes or the same shape 'flipped over'.
14. Understand the application of mathematics to everyday situations.
15. Can see shortcuts in the solution of a problem.

Mathematics covers a number of contrasting areas. An ability to work in the abstract, as in algebra, does not necessarily mean a similar ability in handling work that involves spatial awareness. Similar points could be made about other subjects. One could be fairly ordinary in two-dimensional work in art yet be a world-class sculptor. One might be much stronger in oral French than in written work. One could tackle Advanced level biology well and not be anywhere near as good in Advanced level physics as the demands are different.

If you believe that your child is able in a particular subject you may wish to have a look at a checklist. They are contained in a number of books on able children and some LEAs, such as Hampshire, publish collections. Information can be obtained from the National Association for Able Children in Education, PO Box 242, Arnolds Way, Oxford OX2 9FR (www.nace.co.uk). They are also available on government websites; for example www.nc.uk.net/gt

## Case studies

The school may use potted biographies or case studies of famous people, or possibly able ex-pupils, to help teachers to identify able and talented children.

# ALL SORTS OF ABILITIES

In what different ways might your child be regarded as able and talented?

## Gifted and talented

The government has asked schools in the Excellence in Cities initiative to identify 5–10 per cent of their pupils as gifted and talented: two-thirds by academic ability (known as gifted) and one-third from areas such as art (known as talented). This model is rather narrow and many important human abilities are not given sufficient consideration.

Some schools have limited themselves in terms of the model that they have adopted but many others have taken on a wider appreciation of ability.

## A wider model

Based upon the work of Dr Eric Ogilvie for the Schools Council in 1973, many schools, teachers and INSET (in-service training) providers have worked upon a wide range of abilities. They would include:

- physical talent
- creativity
- visual and performing abilities
- presentational skills
- negotiating skills
- self-awareness
- problem-solving skills
- high intelligence

- sporting prowess
- mechanical ingenuity
- organizational skills
- outstanding leadership
- well-developed social awareness
- strong appreciation of logic
- decision-making ability.

## The underlying principles of such a model

1. It is wide not narrow and not based solely on IQ.
2. It is inclusive not exclusive.
3. It recognizes that all facets of human ability are of equal value, or, in other words, it is just as important to be a good leader as to be good at mathematics, a good negotiator as to be good at English, to have a good social awareness as to be good at science – no more and no less.

## Why is a wider model important?

- For children, it gives many routes to success, thus giving more of them a stake in their school. Success and recognition in one area so often lead to greater confidence, participation and success more generally.

- For schools, it helps to create an ethos in which it is 'cool' to succeed. A wider model also helps to reduce the bullying of academically able pupils for they are just one part of a wider success story.

- For society, it assists availability of the many skills, talents and abilities that are required. In the trouble spots of the world, leadership and negotiating skills are at a premium. Similar skills are also highly valued by companies and businesses.

## Multiple intelligences

Many schools and teachers use the theory of multiple intelligences, as developed by Howard Gardner. This is an alternative, wider model that originally defined seven intelligences and now has an eighth added:

| | |
|---|---|
| Linguistic | a facility for languages |
| Mathematical and logical | ability to sequence, to see order, to solve problems logically |
| Visual and spatial | problem solving by visualization, conceiving three-dimensional objects, good with visual data |
| Musical | at home with tones, rhythms and musical patterns |
| Interpersonal | the skills to work well with other people |
| Intrapersonal | good understanding about one's self |
| Kinesthetic | practical and performing skills |
| Naturalist | at home in, and sensitive to, the natural environment. |

Most children have a jagged profile with strengths and weaknesses across the multiple intelligences. Not many children have a 'high plateau' or great ability across all the multiple intelligences. School subjects cut across the boundaries. Mathematics, for instance, involves visual and spatial as well as mathematical and logical intelligence, thus supporting the view that a child can be able in some parts of a subject and not others.

Avoid a narrow view of ability that is dominated by academic prowess. If your child displays other abilities and talents they are equally valuable and should be encouraged. Society needs the full range of such abilities and talents; carers, leaders and negotiators are vital to our general well-being.

# THE CENTRAL PLACE OF THINKING SKILLS

## Content

Like all children, able pupils have to deal with facts, figures and large specified areas of content. These are laid down for teachers in guidelines such as the national curriculum, the Literacy Framework and the Numeracy Framework. Preparation has to be made for SATs and for examination at GCSE, Advanced level and for various vocational qualifications.

The danger is that too important an emphasis is placed on content. Lessons can then become a rush to complete topics and modules of work. Much content remains unused by the learner after leaving school. It has been covered but, in many ways, it is not what is important in the long term.

What does your able child need to be equipped with in the long term?

The answer is:  **THINKING SKILLS**

## Thinking skills

There are different ways of looking at thinking skills. One important approach is to look at the work of an educationalist called Allan Bloom and those who adopted his work.

## Comprehension and knowledge

These are the lower-order thinking skills. They involve remembering things that have been learned and showing a basic understanding of the work. They are important because children have to work from facts and they have to memorize information for tests and examinations. However, the key word here is basic – the understanding is shallow and it does not really help when tackling other areas of work.

## Application

This might be termed a middle-order thinking skill. Children have learned something and application involves transferring this knowledge to other examples. Teachers use this method a good deal.

## Analysis, synthesis and evaluation

These are the higher-order thinking skills and they are of paramount importance in the education of able and talented children. The government has quite rightly stressed these skills in the information sent to schools involved in the Excellence in Cities initiative.

Analysis involves understanding how parts relate to the total picture. Operations such as investigating, comparing, contrasting and putting into groups are involved.

Synthesis leads to working with several sources of information at the same time and reworking the data into something new. This is a much more complex and demanding way of working than being able to deal singly with individual items, as in comprehension.

Evaluation involves judging a situation in relation to certain criteria. Forming an opinion is critical to many areas of schoolwork and to success at work after school.

These three higher-order thinking skills are vital to the well-being of able children. They go beyond simple understanding and assist the child in approaching new situations with confidence, as transferability is involved.

## The personal view of an historian

The author has history as his main subject at degree level. Much content has been learned for examinations. What is it that makes him valuable to potential employers if he is a good historian? The answer is certainly not that he could say what Gustavus Adolphus of Sweden did at a certain point, but rather that he has a grasp of the higher-order thinking skills of analysis, synthesis and evaluation so that many pieces of information on a problem can be considered and used collectively to come to a reasoned judgement. These skills are of value the world over and assist in dealing with situations in private life.

## Other ways of looking at thinking skills

Some people look at individual items rather than grouped titles such as analysis and synthesis. Some important areas are:

- making predictions
- sequencing information
- classifying information into appropriate groups
- distinguishing fact from opinion
- detecting bias in evidence
- testing an hypothesis fairly
- prioritizing several alternatives
- making a critical assessment

- designing to meet certain criteria
- supporting ideas with evidence
- understanding cause and effect
- forming general rules from specific examples.

## Logical thinking and lateral thinking

Logical thinking is very important in solving problems of many types. It involves a step-by-step progression along a logical route until a conclusion is reached. However, the obvious way forward does not always work. It was the internationally known thinker, Edward de Bono, who promoted the idea of lateral thinking – going sideways to look differently at a problem. Often a variety of possible answers emerge and they can be examined for strengths and weaknesses.

Higher-order thinking skills are vital to able children. The ability to think in different ways is an enormous asset, at school and beyond.

 Try to encourage your child to use thinking skills as often as possible, and to value the more complex working involved. This takes more attention at first but it is crucial to success in the long term.

## CHALLENGE FOR PROGRESS

'Only those who risk going too far can possibly know how far they can go.'

T. S. Eliot

This T. S. Eliot quote was printed on a poster of the planets, and it is a really important philosophy for able and talented children and their parents and carers. Reports and surveys over many years have highlighted the problem that able children are not consistently challenged sufficiently.

What happens to able children when they get almost everything correct and they do not meet failure, either generally or in a particular subject?

As a result:

- ❑ They get on an A-grade treadmill that places unnecessary pressure upon them.
- ❑ They might become intellectually idle, so that when they do eventually face more difficult work they have not got the drive and determination required.
- ❑ They sometimes fail to develop good working habits and learning strategies.

Possible consequences:

- ❑ Many cases have been recorded where able children do not fail significantly until the age of 17 or 18, or even older, and when they do fail they have a nervous breakdown. Failure is not within their experience and, therefore, they cannot deal with it. For instance, one 17-year-old boy had taken in his stride everything before him until his driving test, which he failed. The result was that not only did he give up driving for the next two years, but also that he 'went into his shell' generally.
- ❑ Some very able students going to university, who should get a really good qualification, finish with a poor degree or no degree. Up to this point, nothing has really challenged them. They have not needed to develop the learning strategies that their relatively less able peers have had to use.

*'Nine out of ten of my experiments fail and that is considered a pretty good record amongst scientists.'*

Sir Harold Kroto

So said Sir Harold Kroto, Nobel Prize-winning chemist. Here is one of the greatest scientists in the world embracing the philosophy of failure along the way to notable success.

Failure is not to be avoided at all costs. Too much is destructive but a complete absence is unhelpful and unhealthy. The fear of failure can inhibit progress and exceptional work.

 Make sure that your able child realizes that not all failure is bad. Failure through lack of effort or lack of concentration needs to be tackled, but failure as a result of adventurous thinking is one of the ingredients of success at the highest level. Recognize, with your able child, that the only people who never fail are those who do nothing or those who do 'Mickey Mouse' easy things, which does not ultimately help them nor anybody else.

## The 20/20 mentality

Part of this discussion about challenge, failure and progress is what might be termed the 'twenty-out-of-twenty mentality'. Of course, it is good to get top marks on some occasions. However, if an able child gets full marks much of the time there is only one sensible conclusion to reach – the work is too easy for the child and there is not sufficient challenge.

*'Stuck? Good, now you can really learn something!'*

This was the provocative message on a poster on the classroom wall of a teacher quoted by Professor John MacBeath on an in-service day for teachers in Newcastle upon Tyne some four or five years ago. What is the point of repeating what you can already do well and easily? The able child needs to move on, to progress.

**Stuck?**
Good, now you can really learn something!

 Parents and carers can make an invaluable contribution by making sure that their able children are not so frightened to make mistakes that they become unambitious in their work and therefore fail to achieve what they are capable of doing. If your able child starts getting lower marks, do not assume that this necessarily means a worse performance. Teachers could be put off setting more challenging work if it produces an unfavourable reaction.

# DIFFERENT WAYS OF WORKING

What different teaching methods and forms of organization might the school use in its provision for your able and talented child?

## Grouping policy

There are three main forms of grouping for you to be aware of:

### Streaming

In this system children are placed in the top group for all subjects. Entry to that top group is often through selection on performance in subjects such as English and mathematics. There are a number of concerns here. Research and observation show that the majority of able children are not able 'across the board'. There are genuine all-rounders for whom streaming would work. However, most able children are able in particular subjects or even certain parts of subjects. Streaming results in some children in the top group not being the best in all of them. Conversely, some children who are the most able in one, or in a small number of subjects, do not get into the top group. This mismatch is a considerable worry.

There is also a concern when a school places a child on the able and talented register only if there are very positive reports from at least five subjects. Surely real ability in a single subject requires recognition and suitable provision.

You may have no say in the decision of a school to use streaming, but you do need to be aware of two potential problems. If your child has been placed in the top group, he or she might well struggle in certain subjects. Understanding, encouragement and support are required from parents and carers if this is the case. If your child is able, but not necessarily in the areas regarded as the keys to selection, and, therefore, he or she is not placed in the top group, a careful watch is needed to make sure that appropriate opportunities are available in the subjects where his or her abilities lie.

## Setting

In this system children are placed into groups by ability but subject by subject. As a consequence, a child could be in the top set for some subjects but not for all of them. This overcomes the problems highlighted in streaming. The government has encouraged greater use of setting in the belief that the majority of teachers feel more comfortable with not having too big a spread of ability within a single group. Schools differ in how much setting they use and there are also variations between subjects. Mathematics is frequently the earliest area to set often followed by modern foreign languages. English is set in some schools but certainly not all. Humanities is later to set or does not set at all.

There are three potential problems to look out for:

1. The methods used to place children into sets are vital to its success. The identification section of this book has explained that mathematics is much more than just computation. So, if computation is used as the sole consideration for choosing the top set, some children, able in other areas of mathematics, might be overlooked.

2. There should be flexibility about the setting so that movement is still possible. Performance by children does change over a period of time. It might be necessary to promote some pupils to the top set. Unless the top set is allowed to grow far too big, this will require the demotion of other children.

 Parents and carers like to see their children in the top set. Being put wrongly in the top set is a very uncomfortable and damaging place for a child to be. Don't pressure your child to remain in the top group just for the sake of it. A child who really struggles is likely to be very unhappy. If you are disappointed that your child has not made the top set in a particular subject, and you believe that he or she has the ability to be there, look for assurances that the situation is not cast in concrete and that future movement is possible.

3. Perhaps most importantly of all, the children in the top set should not be provided for uniformly. The top set will contain a range of ability, especially in non-selective city schools. Three or four truly outstanding children will need greater challenge than some other members of the top set.

 Understand that any set, including the top set, is not an homogeneous group. It will contain a range of abilities. If your child is very able indeed, look for work to be provided beyond the tasks that the majority in the top set are given.

## Mixed ability

Here, children in a group or a subject have differing levels of ability. Able pupils work alongside those who are not so strong. The teacher needs to avoid pitching the lessons at the middle of the group and has to support those with weaknesses while, at the same time, looking to challenge the most able children. The advantage is that the teacher knows from the outset that the group is mixed in ability and that more demanding work is needed for the most able. Unfortunately, practice is not always based upon that principle.

 If your able child is placed in a mixed-ability group good individual provision can be made, but look out for any lack of challenge that can result from uniform treatment of such a group.

## Methods of organizing the provision

Again, there are three main forms to consider. The names are used in differing ways so that what is important is not so much the title but the principles behind the method and the consequences of using each.

### Extension within the same topic

Able children often have the facility to master a new technique or skill quickly. They show, from the first group of questions tackled, that they understand. They do not need to keep doing 'more of the same'.

- One method of appropriate provision is to extend the work by setting more complicated questions on the same area or to require deeper research on the topic. Thus, if the group is working on fractions, then those who answer the first examples quickly and well move on to more complicated examples.

- An extension task may well involve able pupils creating their own versions of something that they have been answering. Pairing two definitions of different meanings of the same word from a list is the main task in the author's 'Bark Up the Wrong Tree' (*Challenging Resources for Able and Talented Children*). 'To evade an issue' and 'A soft sweet made from butter, cream and sugar' both lead to the word 'fudge'. Words like this are known as homographs and are covered in the Literacy Framework. For the extension task, able children are invited to find their own homographs and to write separate definitions to define the different meanings. These can then be placed into a mixed-up list so that other pupils can sort them into appropriate pairs. Of course, the main task on homographs in this exercise can already be regarded as extension work to what most children would be asked to do on the topic, as laid down in the Literacy Framework.

In this way, able pupils are challenged by extension tasks that are based upon the normal material of the lesson. There are no other consequences in terms of organization.

## Acceleration

Acceleration involves able children going ahead of their peers along the syllabus. In extreme cases, children can jump a school year and be moved out of their peer group. In some cases this results in early entry for examinations. For instance, a child in Year 9 might take a GCSE examination two years early. Each summer the tabloid newspapers run dramatic stories of much younger children who have secured top grades in GCSE examinations. Acceleration can take place in individual subjects as well as more generally.

Parents and carers should be aware that the government encourages acceleration and it is one of the targets set for Excellence in Cities areas. Such a method does provide a clear source for statistical data. However, the report of a seminar held at the Royal Society in May 2000 called 'Acceleration or Enrichment', and concerning the top 10 per cent in school mathematics, was less than enthusiastic. A group of leading mathematicians voiced considerable concerns. They felt that 'acceleration of individuals must be handled with great caution' and that 'major acceleration often has unanticipated disadvantages for pupils' long-term development'.

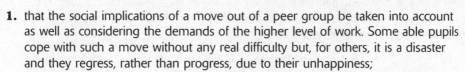

Sensible guidelines for acceleration might well take note of the following 'rules' or considerations:

1.  that the social implications of a move out of a peer group be taken into account as well as considering the demands of the higher level of work. Some able pupils cope with such a move without any real difficulty but, for others, it is a disaster and they regress, rather than progress, due to their unhappiness;

2.  that able pupils taking examinations early are likely to secure the same high grades that they would achieve through normal entry. It would seem pointless to get a 'C' early rather than an 'A' later;

3.  that the enjoyment of the course is not jeopardized seriously due to the reduction of time available. There is a danger that pupils have to move so quickly that rapid absorption of content detracts from the learning and interest;

4.  that there are planned, sensible next stages once acceleration has occurred. There is no point in taking an examination early if no appropriate follow-up is available. This also means that all the partners in able children's education need to co-operate and communicate. Acceleration at the primary school, for example, has important implications for the secondary school and beyond.

 *A decision to accelerate your able and talented child is likely to involve you as parents and carers. Do not be 'flattered' by such a proposal without careful consideration of the personality and emotional maturity of your child, the wishes of the child and the consequences of the acceleration in terms of grades, pleasure in learning and what will follow.*

## Enrichment

Enrichment can be regarded as any activity beyond that carried out by the majority of children. This can involve challenging and exciting material outside the normal syllabus. There are many such areas in mathematics – for instance, outside the Numeracy Framework and the national curriculum – which can provide wonderful learning opportunities, together with great enjoyment. They are also likely to lead to a wider understanding of the whole subject. Different ways of approaching work may also be regarded as enrichment.

Some confusion arises from the fact that extension within a topic can also be seen as enrichment in that it is outside the main body of learning undertaken by the majority of children. The terms 'extension' and 'enrichment' are used interchangeably by some teachers.

Acceleration is fundamentally different from extension within a topic or enrichment in that it results in more fundamental organizational changes and potentially longer-term consequences for the children involved.

## Enrichment courses

Many able and talented children are invited to attend enrichment courses within their own school, or together with children from other schools on 'cluster days' or in summer schools. There are a number of potential benefits:

- coming into contact with children of like mind and similar talents;
- an opportunity to be oneself, as other children are unlikely to be abusive about being able;
- the chance to work for different, and sometimes longer, time periods;
- often there is a residential component that adds challenge and opportunities;
- the hard, but important, realization that there are other people as good, if not better, at a particular activity. This is very important for children who might be regarded as 'big fish in small ponds';
- the chance to tackle new and exciting challenges;
- the likelihood of more teamwork and collaboration than is the norm in many schools.

What features should parents and carers hope to see for their able and talented children within enrichment courses?

- ☑ The activities are significantly different from normal schoolwork.
- ☑ There is a variety of teaching and learning methods.
- ☑ Real challenge is clearly evident. No participant should be 'getting everything correct'.
- ☑ Participants should go away 'having grown' in attitude and/or skills.
- ☑ The courses should be thoroughly enjoyable.

## Preferred learning styles and able children

Able children, like all children, have different preferred learning styles. Some benefit by visual inputs: they use pictures rather than words to learn and understand. Others profit by communicating with and learning by sound: they are said to have an auditory preference. Another group are said to be kinesthetic learners: they enjoy physical activities and practical methods.

There is much talk of VAK (visual, auditory and kinesthetic). Many teachers have been on training courses to help them deliver lessons in a variety of ways in order to play to different preferred learning styles. Books on the subject are common in staff in-service libraries. All of this is helpful and likely to increase the pool of talent by giving children more varied opportunities to demonstrate their abilities. However, where able children are concerned, there still needs to be a real challenge as well as varied inputs. For instance, a visual approach may suit certain children but some visual material could fail to challenge able pupils. The same is true of other preferred learning styles.

There are also individual preferences for physical conditions. Some children like a warm room, others a cooler temperature. Silence is important for some, but a musical background is helpful to others. The optimum amount of light varies. Moving around assists some children while others stay still for long periods. Modern research has challenged the stereotype of sitting concentrating at a desk in quiet conditions with strong light.

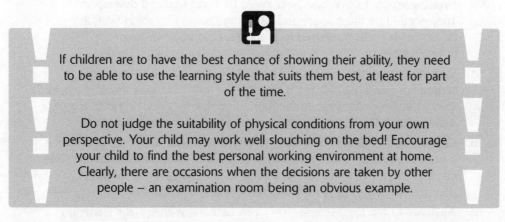

If children are to have the best chance of showing their ability, they need to be able to use the learning style that suits them best, at least for part of the time.

Do not judge the suitability of physical conditions from your own perspective. Your child may work well slouching on the bed! Encourage your child to find the best personal working environment at home. Clearly, there are occasions when the decisions are taken by other people – an examination room being an obvious example.

On enrichment courses, different participants 'star' at different times, as the nature of the activity changes. With a good variety of inputs and outcomes, all children would get the chance to demonstrate their ability.

Work with your able child to discover his or her preferred learning style. When there is a choice, encourage him or her to present answers in the most suitable way. However, do realize that often the outcome is not negotiable, as in many tests and examination situations.

## The general needs of able children

Able and talented children are very different from each other – there is no stereotype. Despite this, there are a number of general needs in terms of provision that are common to the majority of them which are well worth bearing in mind.

- **Less practice at tasks.** When able children have proved their ability to handle a task, technique or method well, they should not be asked to do more examples of the same standard. This is demotivating, pointless and a waste of their time.

- **Sufficient open-ended material.** Able and talented children can only display their ability if enough tasks allow responses of different sophistication, standard and perception.

- **Less detailed instruction.** In curriculum areas where they are strong, able and talented children do not need too much 'scaffolding'. They are able to succeed without too much initial instruction.

- **An appropriate starting point.** At the start of a 'new' topic, some able pupils already have a substantial amount of knowledge and understanding. There is no point in spending time on what they already know. When children first start school, they go with very different previous experiences and existing skills. An able child should never be required to go backwards.

- **More participation in their own learning.** Numerous Ofsted inspection reports complain that in many schools there is not sufficient pupil participation in their own learning. Able and talented children, especially, have the insight to plan how work could be continued and developed. They need to be given space and encouragement to do so. In Scottish documentation this is referred to as differentiation by independence or responsibility.

- **Less steps than the average.** If it takes six steps for the average child to accomplish a task but only three steps for the able child, why should the able child waste his or her time on the three steps that they don't need to comply with everybody else? Jumping steps saves time and prevents frustration.

- **Contact with children of similar ability and talent.** On some occasions it is very beneficial for able and talented children to come together and to 'fire off each other'. This does not necessarily mean setting for all subjects, but it does require some opportunities to work with like peers.

- **Abstract tasks.** Despite what has been said about kinesthetic learning in a previous part of the book, many able children respond well to abstract tasks. They can be found in various areas of schoolwork. In English, proverbs have a more general meaning than the specific example. 'Don't put all your eggs in one basket' is about much more than eggs and baskets. It is, more generally, about spreading risks. Many stories have a meaning beyond the literal or the obvious and able children tend to deal well with symbolism, allegories and higher levels of meaning. In mathematics there is the whole area of algebra where $x$ and $y$ stand for something else. In chemistry one could include symbols and chemical equations. The Scottish 5–14 curriculum guidelines on science talk of an increasing understanding of abstract ideas and principles. In humanities subjects, such as history and politics, able pupils demonstrate a greater facility to deal with terms, for example the difference between law and justice. Codes, too, are very useful tools for able children to work with, as something stands for something else.

o **The opportunity to take risks in an organized way.** Able and talented children need to feel safe and cared for but they also require intellectual challenge. A mistake is not the end of the world. Taking risks is part of growing and realizing what the able and talented child is capable of.

Be aware of the above general needs. Try to see the work that your able child is set at school and for homework in the context of these needs. In organizing games and leisure activities during childhood, try to play to these particular qualities.

# THE GOLDEN COMPONENT THAT IS TIME

Are time considerations different for your child because he or she is able and talented? Is there time for your able child to tackle exciting and interesting tasks that challenge?

Time is the modern preoccupation. Everyone complains of too much to do and too little time to do it in. They feel that they are 'working against the clock'. We hear that 'time is of the essence'. Some schools argue that curriculum guidelines contain so much content that there is no time to do anything else and that, although they would wish to organize exciting learning situations, there is no time to do so.

## Three steps to gain time

1. In many subjects, able children make time by completing the standard tasks quickly and well.

2. At the start of a new topic, some able children already know at least some of the material.

3. Able pupils do not need to go through all the steps required by many of the rest of the class.

If these three principles are applied then, in most subjects, able and talented children make time that is then available for more challenging and enjoyable tasks.

*NOTE:* There are some areas, however, where this is not the case. In art, for instance, able pupils may well take longer over an assignment because they produce a more sophisticated response. This is why art enrichment courses tend to work longer sessions, including late into the evening, so that there is no time constraint.

## A waste of time

The greatest waste of time is when able and talented children are asked to do 'more of the same' when they have already shown a high level of competence. Any amount of time can be used up in that way. There are other examples of wasting the time of able children, such as doing a second neater version or 'colouring it in nicely'. This should not be confused with the benefits from considered redrafting of written work in English lessons.

## Study skills to gain time

There is nothing more time-consuming than copying out unnecessary and irrelevant material. Study skills and advanced reading skills can save a great deal of time. 'Skimming' and 'scanning', for instance, allow the extraction of relevant data quickly and economically.

 Encourage your able and talented child to develop good study skills and advanced reading skills so that time is used to its best value and time gained can be given to exciting, challenging tasks.

 How much time should an able and talented child be working?

Clearly this will increase as they get older and demands of courses rise. Practice time, for instance, for music and sport will also grow for those who have a talent in those areas. Guidelines will be given to parents and carers from schools, teachers and coaches.

## Two important considerations

◻ All children, including those who are able and talented, need leisure time. Domination by work or practice is unhealthy in the long term. A reasonable balance has to be maintained.

◻ Many able and talented children would resent a situation in which they were expected to work for much longer hours than other children, just because they were deemed to have high ability or talent. This is a factor that could lead some children not to want to be identified as able and talented. These children should not be working longer but smarter. They should not be wasting time on repetition and steps that they do not need. This is a much more acceptable 'contract' for able and talented children to contemplate. This does not preclude voluntary attendance at special activities for interest and pleasure.

Should able and talented children always be working quickly and urgently?

There are times when it is beneficial to work at pace. The capacity to work urgently is valuable in many situations. There are time deadlines in tests, examinations and tasks in the world of work. Yet some tasks and decisions need time for reflection. A balance between times of urgency and time for reflection is required.

## Span of concentration

Some tasks can be completed quickly and in a short time, but some require a much longer time. Your children live in a sound-bite society of little attention and concentration. We are increasingly seeing short, snappy outcomes.

It is vitally important that your able and talented child develops a span of concentration and the ability to focus attention. If not, many important tasks, achievements and attainments will be out of reach.

Encourage your child to be involved in some lengthy activities where a good span of concentration is required.

## Parents' and carers' time

Many parents and carers live in a world of pressure and deadlines; the pace is frantic at times. Working hours for many people are long and demanding. Able children, like all children, benefit from quality time with their parents and carers. Indeed, one of the characteristics of many able children is that they prefer time with older children and parents or carers than with their own age group.

 Do everything possible to spend quality time with your able child – to talk, play games, go on trips and outings, share enthusiasms, give encouragement, take an interest, and act as a sounding board for ideas.

# HOMEWORK

Able and talented children differ considerably in terms of personality and character. Some are hard-working and conscientious; others are lazy and try to avoid making much effort. Those that are idle will not welcome homework of any sort. Others will not object to homework unless it seems to be a waste of time.

 What homework is suitable for your able child?

## Methods that work

A number of different principles are suitable. They are described here by the technical term by which they will be known by teachers and then their meaning explained.

| Technical term | Meaning |
|---|---|
| Differentiation by outcome or response | All children are given the same homework, but it is open-ended enough to be answered at different levels. 'What were the causes of the First World War?' can bring responses of varying quality and insight. |
| Differentiation by task | Different tasks are set for pupils' homework so that able children are faced with more challenging and demanding work. |
| Differentiation by text or resource | All the children study the same topic, but the books and resources used operate at varying levels of difficulty. This method is often used to assist differentiation by outcome. Research for future topics figures here. |
| Differentiation by content | Able pupils who have finished the normal work are given material outside the usual syllabus to provide interest and challenge. |
| Differentiation by independence or responsibility | When they have completed a module of work, able pupils are encouraged to develop their own ideas further. |

*NOTE:* These principles are those which can also be employed within lessons.

There are a number of sensible ways of setting homework for able pupils so that they are properly challenged.

## One damaging method

Homework is sometimes used to consolidate understanding of a technique or method. Able pupils often master a new topic quickly and easily. They show this by the completion of correct answers within a few minutes. Doing more examples of the same standard for homework may be necessary for some members of the class but it is inappropriate for able children as it causes boredom, dissatisfaction and sometimes a tendency to go more slowly. Additional examples at a more difficult level are, of course, a different matter.

 Take an interest in your able child's homework. Make available a suitable workspace. Look to see that homework tasks are challenging enough and be especially wary about repetitive tasks that are too easy.

# PRESENTATION AND SPELLING

The ideal situation is when an able child completes work of high quality neatly, beautifully presented and with no spelling errors. When this occurs, life is very simple.

How important are presentation and spelling for able and talented children?

The obvious answer is that everybody should strive to make them as good as possible but there are some important factors to consider.

## Being seduced by superficial appearance

We tend to be impressed by neatness and good presentation, while a lengthy response tends to attract praise. There are, however, many occasions when children write at length and with accuracy and yet the answer lacks quality and real understanding. Remember that many people with great minds, who have made important contributions, were untidy; they certainly would not have won any prizes for presentation.

On their own, good presentation and accurate spelling do not signify high quality.

If children do not spell well, does it mean that they cannot be able?

Poor spelling is one of the features of work done by children who struggle in the classroom. However, there are many examples of poor spellers who have major abilities and talents. They are not ruled out as being able because of poor spelling. They have a weakness and everybody should try to make improvements.

An able child, who shows great understanding and displays really good ideas, will not prosper if all that he or she receives is criticism about his or her spelling.

 Encourage clear presentation, appropriate length and accurate spelling. Work with the school to remedy weaknesses but do not see presentation and spelling as all-important. Instead, try to put them into a wider context. Praise good understanding and quality ideas while cajoling gently any improvements that are desirable.

# CHANGING SCHOOLS

Changing schools, or transition, creates a situation that can result in problems for able and talented children, unless real care is taken and communication is good.

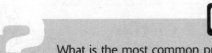

What is the most common problem that occurs when an able child moves into the next phase of education?

Overwhelmingly, the answer is repetition of work due to a lack of understanding as to the level already reached by the able and talented child. There is a tendency to underestimate what younger, able children are capable of doing. A cautious approach is normally taken, as the 'receiving' school likes to prove for itself exactly what the new pupils can do. This can result in able children being asked to do work that they have completed successfully some time previously. The problem seems to be particularly prevalent in mathematics. Repetition can easily lead to boredom, disenchantment and possibly bad behaviour. At the least, it is a waste of precious time. Many schools do take great care to communicate information about pupils leaving them but, even so, problems continue on many occasions.

In advance of changing school, take every opportunity to tell the 'receiving' school the standard reached in an area of high ability or talent.

Be particularly vigilant, during the first half term in a new school, to see that work set provides an adequate challenge. If you are concerned make contact with the form tutor or able child co-ordinator.

Is there anything that particularly applies to moving school in an Excellence in Cities area?

There is the possibility that a child identified in the gifted and talented cohort at primary school might not be in a similar position in the secondary school. This can be quite perplexing for the parents of that child. The reason is due to statistics. Excellence in Cities' schools are asked to identify a cohort of up to 10 per cent. Primary schools have different intakes and one school's 10 per cent is rather different from another's 10 per cent. This is what causes the discrepancy at secondary school.

What matters is not whether your child is in the 10 per cent but rather that your child is properly challenged at the correct ability level. Many Excellence in Cities' schools recognize that they have more than 10 per cent of their pupils who can be regarded as able and talented. Providing that they make appropriate provision, inclusion in the 10 per cent is not important.

# LOOKING AFTER YOUR ABLE CHILD

Your child is not just an intellect on legs or a talent. Without concern for the whole child the ability or talent will not flourish.

## Social and emotional development

Decisions should never be taken solely on the basis of the intellect or performance capacity; the social and emotional needs of the child need to be considered. Able children, despite their talents, are still children and they need to be treated as such. Moving out of peer group, to be accelerated through a syllabus, works for some children but it turns out to be a disaster for others who are equally able. Happiness and a sense of well-being are important considerations. There is no 'blueprint' as able and talented children are all very different and their needs are varied. A successful way of dealing with one able and talented child can be entirely inappropriate for another.

 When taking decisions, the parents and carers of able and talented children need to take into account the social and emotional needs of the individual child.

## Some pitfalls to avoid

The huge majority of parents and carers, including those of able and talented children, want what is best for their children. But is it always clear what is best?

There are some pitfalls to try to avoid so as to serve your child's best interests, including:

 Avoid living out your ambitions through your child's life. The result may well be too much pressure and plans that are not really what the child wants to do.

 Look to a partnership with the school rather than a running battle; this includes not browbeating staff with test scores and comments from an educational psychologist. You and your able child have rights, but co-operation is always better than confrontation.

 Prevent able children from feeling that their value lies only in their ability or talent rather than in themselves as people. Able pupils sometimes tell teachers that they resent being treated as examination fodder, bolstering up results and league-table positions.

 Avoid taking a narrow view of marks and results. Full marks for inappropriate and unchallenging tasks are not significant. It is far better to get fewer marks for a really difficult piece of work.

 Try not to be too overprotective of talents. One understands, to some extent, a policy of no physical sport to protect the hands of a promising pianist, but is it really in the best interests of the whole child?

Avoid ignoring the interests of other parents, carers and children in your justifiable search for what is right for your able and talented child. This book tries to equip parents and carers of able pupils with the understanding and information to carry out a meaningful dialogue with the school. Central to the book is the duty of schools to provide well for able children. However, they also have a duty to provide equally well for other children.

## Some problems faced by able and talented children

> Many able and talented children are very contented and happy, and are well integrated into the school community.

Despite the important message above, there are problems faced by some able and talented children that parents and carers should be aware of:

- Bullying of able children is not uncommon. Name-calling terms are used such as 'prof', 'boff' and 'keener'. Intimidation and physical bullying may also take place. The danger is that the able children underachieve so as to avoid the displeasure of the bullies.
- Able children can 'dampen down' their talents to conform with others. A minority are a little eccentric and can attract unfavourable attention from other children.
- Boredom is not uncommon if work is repetitive and unchallenging.
- Frustration occurs when the quality of the ideas and plans outruns the skills to deliver those ideas. Temper and poor behaviour could be the consequence.
- Able and talented children are tempted to use their own way to tackle a piece of work rather than follow class instructions. This can lead to difficulty with the teacher, unless he or she is understanding and sympathetic.
- Some able and talented children might appear as a threat to some teachers because of the advanced ability that they possess, perhaps in excess of the teacher's ability. This can cause an uneasy relationship.
- Sleeping less than their peers is a characteristic of some able children, but its frequency might have been exaggerated. Where it is a reality, other members of the family might be disturbed.
- Some able and talented children are bored with the company of their peers and their interests differ. They prefer the company of older children and adults. This can produce an unfavourable reaction from peers.
- Precocious behaviour, especially by very young children, sometimes jars on other children and adults. A dislike can be engendered even though this is grossly unfair.

- Not all able and talented children are good at collaboration and working in teams. They prefer to work on their own, which can cause disputes.

- One way used by teachers to deal with the able child is to set individual work away from other children. Done too much, this isolates able children who need contact with others and a share of the teachers' attention.

- Rewards systems find it difficult to deal with able pupils and some schools acknowledge that less able children receive more merits than anybody else in order to motivate them. Able children may well resent not receiving appropriate rewards. They should not receive commendation just because their work is better than average, but to exclude them from the rewards system of their school is unfair.

- If children abuse their ability and talents to behave badly, they must expect punishment. However, able and talented children sometimes feel unjustly dealt with because they are punished for advancing their views and skills when it is seen, incorrectly, as cheek.

 **When dealing with the consequences of these problems, keep in mind the root causes so that you can support your able child in an appropriate way.**

# ABLE UNDERACHIEVERS

Able and talented children vary considerably in terms of their personality and characteristics. There is a stereotype of the able child being hard-working, conscientious and teacher-pleasing. The reality, however, can be very different. It is particularly frustrating if you believe that your child is able and talented but that he or she is underachieving.

How might we spot underachievement?

Just as there are subject checklists, there are also lists to help identify able underachievers through examples of typical behaviour. Points to look for include:

- The general standard of work or performance is not very high but there are odd flashes of brilliance that give a clue as to what could be achieved.

- Oral work is promising but the standard of answer is markedly different when a written response is required.

- A piece of work starts off well but then the standard tails off dramatically.

- Ability is clear when dealing with short tasks but lack of sustained concentration reduces the standard when longer tasks are involved.

- Application is very selective. A good effort is made for a minority of tasks in which the child has a real interest but this effort is not normally the case.

- Ability is misused. For instance, perceptive questions are asked, but only to cause discomfort for the teacher rather than to get a genuine response.

- The child postpones getting into a task with much unnecessary delay and, once started, much time is wasted in daydreaming.

- Working well in one area where the relationship with the teacher is very good but the effort elsewhere is noticeably less.

How might parents and carers help to
combat underachievement?

The starting point is to try to identify the cause of the underachievement. There can be many different causes and the action needed will vary accordingly.

 The child has an undiscovered physical disability that is causing a problem, such as a hearing difficulty or a sight deficiency. The solution can be as simple as being moved to the front of the classroom.

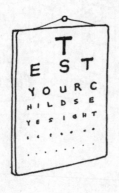

There could be a fear of failure. Some able and talented children are hypercritical of themselves; a piece of work has to be perfect or it is not worth doing at all. The attitude might be commendable in some ways but it can also be very damaging and the drive for perfection leads to procrastination or delay. Parents and carers can help by reducing the pressures of an 'A-grade treadmill'. They need to assist the child to adopt a more realistic approach. Nobody is perfect. Everybody makes mistakes. Sometimes time constraints limit what can be achieved.

 Some able and talented children are lazy. There are even some who see ability as doing as little as possible and getting away with it. Parents, carers and teachers need to be very firm. Real love involves being unpleasant at times.

 Unfortunately, there are times when peer pressure, a youth culture in which it is not 'cool' to succeed, and bullying persuade able and talented children to disguise their strengths and to underachieve rather than get 'on the wrong side' of other children. Parents and carers need to talk to the school so that the problem can be tackled at an institutional level.

 Not all able and talented children possess good organizational skills. As a result, good ideas and answers are left disorganized and are confusing. Parents and carers can help such children, through discussion and good examples, to improve their study skills and their working habits.

 The normal learning 'diet' is unchallenging and able pupils succeed too easily. When they occasionally meet something more demanding, they have lost the necessary intellectual stamina. A shift of balance to a higher level of challenge does ultimately pay dividends, but patience and persistence are required as the change of attitude will not occur immediately.

 There is a very special group of people who have a learning disability but also possess great ability or talent in one or more specific areas. They include autistic children, those with Asperger's syndrome and the many who are dyslexic. It is not uncommon for some children in school to appear on both the special educational needs register and the able and talented register.

Underachievement occurs if provision in all areas, including the one in which there is high ability and talent, is governed by the problems of the learning disability. Parents and carers can remind schools, and other providers, that the difficulty should not exclude challenge in appropriate areas.

Not all able and talented children possess self-confidence and self-belief. They need constant encouragement and support at home to achieve success. It is sometimes those who are brash on the outside who suffer from gnawing internal doubts that can be destructive without support from family and others.

Able and talented children are very different. Some suffer from doubts and weaknesses. The old adage that 'clever children can look after themselves' is far from the truth in many, many cases. A lot of able children do underachieve. Finding the cause is the first step to improving the situation. Avoid pressure and punishment for underachievement – it could make it worse!

# SECTION 2
## GETTING FURTHER ADVICE AND HELP

 First and foremost, keep regular contact with your able child's school via the able and talented co-ordinator, the class teacher, the form tutor, the subject teacher, the head of year or the senior management team. A partnership with the school is the key to good provision. Hopefully this parents' and carers' guide makes you more informed so that you know what to look for and what the issues are.

 Make contact with NAGC (National Association for Gifted Children), Suite 14, Challenge House, Sherwood Drive, Bletchley, Milton Keynes MK3 6DP (telephone 0845 450 0221; email *amazingchildren@nagcbritain.org.uk*; website *www.nagcbritain.org.uk*). This charity is by far the largest organization for the parents and carers of able and talented children. There are activities that can be described as being within three strands. Volunteers, the first strand, run the branches that are spread across the country. Information about them is updated regularly in the NAGC newsletter. Explorers' Clubs organize activities for able children of varying ages. The extent of these activities varies with the size and experience of the branch. Counselling services are available and there is an independent parental support scheme. The second strand is educational. Members have access to a helpline that receives some 2,000 calls and 500 emails a year. Specific research projects are undertaken, sometimes in collaboration with other organizations, on issues such as early years and home-school liaison. In-service opportunities are available at schools or on courses. There is also the production of the *Journal of the NAGC*. The third strand is the youth agency. This is a members' online forum for 11-18 year olds. It was established to handle problems but it now has a more positive outlook as youngsters share ideas. *Muse* is the quarterly magazine that showcases the work of members across the country on topics that engage and inspire them.

 Explore the services and resources made available by NACE (National Association for Able Children in Education), PO Box 242, Arnold's Way, Oxford OX2 9FR (telephone 01865 861879, email *info@nace.co.uk*, website *www.nace.co.uk*). This primarily is the association for professionals working with able children - teachers, headteachers, lecturers and advisers. However, parents and carers can join or purchase resources. Newsletters and a journal keep members informed. There is a helpline service. A great deal of in-service training is provided for teachers and there is an extensive publications list in association with the publishers David Fulton. Two leaflets are sent to parents and carers who request help but more detailed advice is dependent upon membership.

 Look at the activities of the junior members of British Mensa, St John's House, St John's Square, Wolverhampton WV2 4AH (telephone 01902 772771, email *enquiries@mensa.org.uk*, website *www.mensa.org.uk*). They keep in touch through *Bright Sparks* magazine. Junior members have access to the same opportunities as adults - a monthly colour magazine, regional newsletters announcing events, and special interest groups covering art to zoology and everything in-between. Children above ten-and-a-half years old have to take prescribed tests to join. Under that age entry is through a report by an educational psychologist.

 Make contact with other parents and carers who have able and talented children. Many such children are well integrated into their schools and families but others do face problems. Mutual support can be very beneficial. One way to make contact is through the local branch of NAGC (details on page 47).

 Contact a recognized educational psychologist in your area to obtain an independent assessment of your child's abilities and advice on care and provision. Such an assessment can be valuable in discussions with your child's school, providing that it is not used forcefully as a weapon against staff, when it might be counterproductive.

 Look for details of enrichment activities run by the LEA or other group. Check if the LEA has a co-ordinator for able children. Some areas have special centres. For instance, the Brunel Able Children's Education (BACE) Centre, Brunel University, Twickenham Campus, 300 St Margaret's Road, Twickenham TW1 1PT (telephone 020 8891 0121 ext. 2070, email *Valsa.Koshy@brunel.ac.uk*) works with teachers, carries out research, publishes books and curriculum materials and 'supports pupils who exhibit high academic talents by working through their LEAs through masterclasses and enrichment programmes offered through local teachers'.

# Specific subject advice, resources, and help

There follows a series of practical suggestions on how you can help your able and talented child in subject areas, as listed below, that are a particular strength. These cannot be definitive lists but they do provide substantial sets of suggestions that lead to many activities and opportunities.

## SECTION 2 CONTENTS

# ART

■ Share work that is done privately at home with the teachers at school. Create a real partnership.

■ Provide opportunities in as wide a range of media as possible, as a high ability in, for instance, three-dimensional work, such as modelling, sculpture and constructional activities, may not be apparent in the child's two-dimensional work.

■ For young children, make available boxes, crayons, paints, plasticine, card, sticky paper, objects and natural materials such as twigs and leaves. Wallpaper lining paper provides a plentiful and cheap medium on which to draw and paint.

■ Make visits to as many art galleries and museums as possible.

■ Work through the Parents' Teachers' and Friends' Association (PTFA) at school to encourage (and possibly to fund) visits by practising artists.

■ Encourage work from first-hand sources and provide a pocket sketchpad to record experiences spontaneously wherever and whenever. Observation is an important component. Discourage just copying cartoons and pictures.

■ Look to create long periods of time – able artists sometimes take longer on an assignment as they produce a more sophisticated response.

■ Support any opportunities for the child to work alongside others of similar interest and ability. This might be achieved through sessions at galleries and museums, LEA enrichment courses, summer schools and weekend art courses organized by other agencies. A residential experience can be particularly beneficial.

■ For older children, consider additional opportunities through evening classes.

■ Encourage the display of work around the house or outside the home in local libraries, health centres and other public buildings. This 'celebration' is very important. It is particularly powerful if the display also includes the work of established artists.

■ Provide a rich environment with many stimuli to fire the imagination and prompt themes for development.

■ Look out for art competitions for your child to enter, both nationally and locally.

■ Within financial resources, make available a stock of art books and periodicals.

■ Encourage your child to open up work to frank and vigorous comment from teachers and other experts. This can be a sensitive area. Comments during the developmental stage of a piece of work are especially valuable.

■ Give support during tricky times as the able artist will inevitably go through frustrating periods. There will be times when technical ability will lag behind ideas.

■ Be prepared to accept a mess when your child is working at home. Obviously you will want to protect carpets and furniture, but beneficial activities are not always neat and tidy with, for instance, just a piece of paper and a set of coloured pencils.

■ Make sufficient space available for particular activities.

■ Purchase a good-quality sketchbook. Encourage your able and talented child to use this for a variety of materials – collage, textiles, photographs as well as for drawing.

■ Make available a good-quality camera, if financially possible. This gives an immediate route to a composition. A digital camera allows amendment to composition in a creative way.

■ Acquire a set of Magnetic Poetry – Shapes (available from many bookshops). There are 150 pieces in seven different colours. Use these to create abstract compositions in a 'doodling' sort of way. The set would also be of interest to able children with an interest in mathematics.

■ Subscribe to one, or more, of the monthly magazines that are available from newsagents. *The Artist* provides 'inspiration, instruction and practical ideas for all artists'. Its contents include articles, demonstration pieces, techniques, tips, a practical problem-solver feature and news of exhibitions, courses and events. *Leisure Painter* has a painting-project critique, dates for your diary, articles, demonstrations, a beginners' section, a quarterly series on societies such as The Royal Society of Painter–Printmakers and information from art clubs. *A and I Artists and Illustrators* has news and views from the world of art, new art products,

articles, demonstrations, a digital supplement and information on competitions and artists available for demonstrations. All three of these are beautifully illustrated. Some contents follow a similar monthly pattern, while others change from issue to issue.

Encourage your able child to use a specialist dictionary to help build up subject-specific vocabulary. *The Questions Dictionary of Art* by Rob Barnes, suitable for junior and lower secondary pupils, provides comprehensive definitions of words and concepts used in the teaching of art. It can be ordered on 0121 666 7878 or email *sales@questpub.co.uk*. Or, Oxford University Press publishes *The Concise Oxford Dictionary of Art and Artists*. Ask your able child to devise a word game based upon art terms in the dictionary. Alternatively your child can create a crossword where all the answers are art terms. Writing the clues would be particularly useful.

# DRAMA

 Encourage your able and talented child to make full use of drama facilities at school – drama club, lunchtime sessions, studio productions and full school productions.

 Build up a collection of videos or DVDs of productions, or borrow them from a library. Get your child to study various aspects of them, such as performance, set and direction. Watch two productions of the same play and ask your child to make critical comparisons.

 Try to organize work experience at a local theatre when your child is the appropriate age. Getting an inside feel is important.

 Arrange for your child to mix with equally able pupils who have a strong interest in drama. This can be through enrichment courses run by LEAs or other educational organizations.

 Organize a visit to the Theatre Museum, Russell Street, Covent Garden, London WC2E 7PR (free mailing list – family/general news telephone 020 7943 4745, email *tmfamilies@vam.ac.uk*, general information *www.theatremuseum.org*). The galleries, charting the British stage from today back to Shakespeare's time, are brought to life by tour guides who explore the work of star performers, practitioners and their audiences. There are special exhibitions, theatrical make-up demonstrations, costume workshops, a Kids Theatre Club (8–12 years old) on Saturdays, creative activities in Stage Struck (storytelling sessions on the first Saturday of the month), drama sessions for 13–18 year olds in From Display to Performance on Wednesdays during school holidays and special holiday themes during school breaks. There is a workshop programme for groups (telephone 020 7943 4806), some of which is linked to visits to West End shows. In 2002 the Theatre Museum contributed descriptions of all its collections to an electronic portal for UK performing arts collections. At *www.backstage.ac.uk* you can search for material on specific subjects or simply browse through descriptions of the Museum's collections.

🎭 Look for public-speaking competitions for your child to enter. This gives him or her the opportunity for good use of the voice and general performing skills.

🎭 Ask your child to compile a dictionary of theatrical terms. All subjects have specialist vocabulary and drama is certainly no exception.

🎭 Take your child to the theatre for a variety of performances, as many as finances allow. Afterwards, make time for a family discussion. Encourage your child to write a criticism of the performance. Obtain copies of reviews published in newspapers. Hold discussions on whether you agree with what has been written.

🎭 Explore the opportunities provided by The Mousetrap Foundation, 15 New Row, London WC2N 4LD (telephone 020 7836 4388, email *info@mousetrap.org.uk*, website *www.mousetrap.org.uk*). The Mousetrap Foundation creates theatre education and access programmes to ensure that young people, with limited resources or support, have equal opportunities to experience live theatre in London's West End. Top-price tickets are offered at £5 or less. There are also practical resource packs, workshops, meet the actors sessions, and masterclasses with directors, writers and designers. Check to see if your school knows about TheatreWorks that provides classroom projects involving up to eight hours of practical workshops. Envision, devised in partnership with Vocaleyes and the Theatre Museum, provides enhancing theatre visits for blind and partially sighted young people. Subsidized theatre days include tickets to an audio-described play or musical, a workshop at the Theatre Museum, backstage and on-stage tours and a specially commissioned audio-tape cassette.

🎭 Build up a collection of suitable texts or borrow copies from a library. Consult with the school about titles. Look for a variety that cover the various aspects of drama such as *Stage Management: The Essential Handbook* by Gail Pallin, *Theatre Games: A New Approach to Drama Training* by Clive Barker containing many exercises to carry out, *Finding Your Voice* by Barbara Houseman which looks not only at voice-training but also lifestyle issues such as eating. Patsy Rodenburg is a much respected voice expert; she has a number of publications (including books, videos and audio tapes) available through booksellers or specialist outlets such as the National Theatre Bookshop (details below).

🎭 Attend events involving storytellers. Ask your child to tell stories to the family and to enact out stories and poems.

Seek out competition opportunities such as writing or performing in a short play. Many theatres have festivals of new plays. Although not a competition, the Royal National Theatre and Shell promote Connections, 'a celebration of youth theatre'. All Connections' plays are targeted for performance by 11–19 year olds, with cast sizes from seven upwards. The settings are designed to challenge the imagination and inspire creativity. Write Now, developed in partnership between The Mousetrap Foundation (details opposite) and the Donmar Warehouse, is a playwriting programme for A-level students offering them the opportunity to see a staged reading of their ten-minute 'plays' with professional actors, critiqued by a panel of directors and playwrights.

Contact your nearest local professional theatres to find out what youth and education programmes they run, some of which are very extensive and varied. The Bristol Old Vic (King Street, Bristol BS1 4ED, telephone 0117 949 3993, email *education@bristol-old-vic.co.uk*, website *www.bristol-old-vic.co.uk*) runs workshops mixing discussion, demonstration and practical activity, Friday morning fun sessions for the under fives, an associate youth theatre open to 7–21 year olds and a summer theatre course for 11–18 year olds. The Theatre Royal Plymouth (Royal Parade, Plymouth, Devon PL1 2TR, telephone 01752 230377, website *www.theatreroyal.com*) has a resident Young Company, Young Dance Company and Tiny Company (4–7 year olds) that all meet for regular workshop sessions. Their education team commissions new works for young audiences and young performers. There are currently projects for primary schools in collaboration with the Royal National Theatre.

Investigate community theatre in your locality; your local library will carry information. Some community productions are performed in conjunction with a professional theatre such as the New Vic Theatre, Newcastle-under-Lyme and the Northcott Theatre, Exeter.

Buy a set of finger puppets for your young able child. Put in a rogue character that does not sit easily with the others. Ask your child to write a script and to perform the finger-puppet play that results.

Seek out audition opportunities for wider-based groups such as a county youth theatre. This may have to be done via the school.

Take advantage of tours of theatres and talks by professionals, which form part of the programme for most companies. Try to attend after-show discussions with members of the cast or special events connected to particular productions.

Purchase a model theatre and get your child to write a script and perform for family and friends. There is a wonderful selection at Benjamin Pollock's Toyshop, 44 The Market, Covent Garden, London WC2E 8RF (telephone 020 7379 7866) which can be purchased online at *www.pollocks-coventgarden.co.uk*

● Subscribe to *The Stage* which is published every Thursday. This can be done through a newsagent, or there is a subscription service (telephone 01858 438895, email *thestage@subscription.co.uk*, website *www.thestage.co.uk*). Also consider magazines such as *Theatregoer* and *Theatre Record*.

● Consider having a theatre break. Perhaps centre it on Stratford-upon-Avon, and take in the Shakespeare sites. Attend performances in the Royal Shakespeare Theatre and the Swan Theatre. During the Summer Festival it is possible to see several productions during a single week. There are cast discussions, talkbacks after the performances, meetings with the directors and a series of day schools. The Swan Theatre has an extensive shop, including educational materials with an exhibition located above. There is an education programme, including the RSC Play Guides – online resource packs which accompany the plays in the season. Tours around both theatres are available (telephone 01789 403405, email *theatre.tours@rsc.org.uk*). General contact details are Royal Shakespeare Company, Waterside, Stratford-upon-Avon, Warwickshire CV37 6BB (Box Office telephone 0870 609 1110, website *www.rsc.org.uk*).

A very good alternative is a break in London especially involving the Royal National Theatre, South Bank, London SE1 9PX (telephone 020 7452 3400, website *www.nationaltheatre.org.uk*). With three main theatres and productions in rep, a variety of productions can be seen in a week. There is a permanent exhibition of the National's history, called 'Stage by Stage', and also temporary exhibitions. The bookshop has a very extensive specialist theatre stock (telephone 020 7452 3456, email *bookshop@nationaltheatre.org.uk*). Backstage tours are readily available. 'Platform' presents a programme of talks and events. There is an education programme for young people throughout the year, including youth theatre projects, touring productions, in-service training for teachers and other work in schools.

● Organize visits to law courts, council meetings, public enquiries, special event launches, debates and, indeed, anywhere where people 'perform', to witness drama as it takes place in life.

● Encourage your child to evaluate the contributions of him or herself, and other people, after public performances. A sensible balance is required between complacency and over-severe self-criticism.

● Obtain a copy of *100 + Ideas for Drama* by Anna Scher and Charles Verrall. This is a book of ideas, based on work at the famous Anna Scher Children's Theatre in London, which can be adapted and developed for any situation. The introduction, 'Who this book is for', includes parents looking for things for their children, and their children's friends, to do. The book is divided into six main sections: Games; The Spoken Word; Warm-ups, Mime and Movement; Characters, Props and Costumes; Situation Drama; and Improvised Plays and Technique.

📑 Explore what is offered locally by theatre schools. Some run courses only in a particular area, while others have facilities over a wide geographical range. One such is Stagecoach Theatre Arts School, The Courthouse, Elm Grove, Walton-upon-Thames, Surrey KT12 1LZ (telephone 01932 254333, website *www.stagecoach.co.uk*), who provide opportunities in drama, singing and dance for children aged four upwards around the world.

📑 Accumulate costumes, clothes and props for a dressing-up box, especially for younger children, to stimulate creativity, imagination and role play.

# ENGLISH

## P LAYING WITH LANGUAGE

Encourage the use of word games, which help in promoting extension of vocabulary and a joy in language. There are specialist publications such as Tony Augarde's *Oxford Guide to Word Games*. General collections of puzzles include a section on word games, as in, for example, the MENSA series. A set of new editions from MENSA includes *Word Puzzles for Kids* by Robert Allen. They have six levels of difficulty: 'Thumb Suckers'; 'Pencil Chewers'; 'Nail Nibblers'; 'Head Bangers'; 'Teeth Grinders'; and 'Aaargh!' Many newspapers have a puzzle page that includes word games.

Support the regular completion of crossword puzzles. Find a standard that is appropriate to start with and then encourage advancement to something more demanding. Crossword puzzles are published by newspapers and magazines, and collections are readily available from bookshops and large newsagents.

Contact The Crossword Club, Coombe Farm, Awbridge, Romsey, Hampshire SO51 0HN, on behalf of older children (telephone 01794 524346, email *bh@thecrosswordclub.co.uk*, website *www.crosswordclub.co.uk*). They run specialized competitions that are very challenging.

Suggest that your able and talented child writes crossword puzzles and word games of his or her own.

Play language-based games as a family, such as Scrabble, Lexicon, Double Quick, Upwords, Dingbats and Wordrop.

- Have available a really extensive dictionary and a lengthy thesaurus; both can provide a treasury of information. They also answer the requirements of curriculum guidelines in English and literacy. Get your child to use them in a challenging way by using a lipogram: where a passage is written without using a particular letter of the alphabet. Choose a short piece of writing of any sort, including a nursery rhyme. Get your child to rewrite it as close to the original meaning without using, for instance, the letter 's' or the letter 'd'. If you want it really challenging make the forbidden letter an 'a' or 'e'!

- Help your child to understand that language does not remain constant but that it is always changing. Ask for two lists to be compiled: one of new words that have entered the language through, for example, the development of computers or the attention paid to environmental issues; and a second list where modern usage of existing words has changed, such as 'wicked' or 'cool'. Take a look at two contrasting texts that highlight this movement in language – *The Oxford Dictionary of New Words* edited by Erin McKean and *Forgotten English* by Jeffrey Kacirk.

- Encourage the exploration of fascinating areas of language such as proverbs, riddles, idioms and similes. Collections can be purchased or borrowed from libraries.

- Make language live by organizing a family walk during which your child collects examples of literary terms, such as onomatopoeia, alliteration, antonomasia and palindromes. Use a book of reference such as *A Concise Oxford Dictionary of Literary Terms* edited by Chris Baldick. Turn it into a treasure hunt if you wish or use a competition format.

# SPEAKING AND LISTENING

- Find quality time to listen to your able and talented child and take part in meaningful discussion with him or her. Encourage debate and reasoned argument. When asked a question by your child, try to avoid hasty, stopgap answers and, instead, reply in a full and thoughtful way. A sustained commitment of this sort will extend language skills and promote thinking skills.

- Organize the opportunity to interview family members and friends.

- Encourage oral presentations and story-telling opportunities.

- Look for formal opportunities for debate and presentation. Libraries and schools often have information about public-speaking competitions.

- Play your own family version of *Just a Minute* where a player has to speak for 60 seconds on a chosen subject without hesitation, repetition or deviation from the subject.

Organize visits to law courts, markets, sales promotions, council meetings, poetry readings, election rallies, chat shows and so on, for your child to hear language used in many contexts and for varying purposes.

 # WRITING

Look out for writing courses organized by LEAs, the National Association for Gifted Children and other organizations. The Arvon Foundation runs highly respected creative writing courses at centres in Devon, Yorkshire, Shropshire and Inverness-shire (details are available on the website *www.arvonfoundation.org*).

Take a balanced view about spelling and presentation. Where there are problems, look for improvement but not so forcibly that your child's desire to write is squashed.

Organize enough time, in a block, to enable sustained extended writing to take place.

The *Young Writer* magazine can be ordered via newsagents or directly from Young Writer, Glebe House, Weobley, Herefordshire HR4 8SD (telephone 01544 318901, email *youngwriter@enterprise.net*, website *www.youngwriter.org*). This specialist magazine appears three times a year and is aimed at writers aged 6–18 years, and is a forum for young people's writing – fiction, non-fiction, prose and poetry. Also, children interview leading authors who pass on advice. There is one major competition in each issue plus other prizes and challenges. There are creative ideas, technical tips, group writing activities and the exploration of areas of interest such as self-publication and word processing. Grammar, idioms and poetic forms are among items that are explained. *Young Writer* is also a debating forum where young writers introduce issues that they feel strongly about. There is also a *Young Writer's Summer Anthology*.

Encourage participation in writers' groups and poetry groups. Peer evaluation is extremely beneficial.

Take advantage of contact with professional writers through festivals, special events and attendance at talks hosted by large bookshops.

Promote keyboard skills so that your child can make the best use of word-processing equipment.

Search out writing competitions through school, libraries, newspapers and elsewhere. *The Times Educational Supplement*, in conjunction with the National Association for the Teaching of English, runs an annual competition called Write Away. Registration is through your child's school.

Provide a sounding board for work in progress so that your child is clear about the purpose of the writing, what the piece sounds like and what its effect is on other people.

- ✍ Support the process of your child checking and redrafting work. A really good piece of writing is unlikely to be produced by just one attempt.

- ✍ Encourage writing of a variety of styles – narrative, explanation, persuasion, evaluation and so on. Look for examples of criticisms of television programmes and plays, accounts of visits, letters on issues to the local newspaper, articles for the school magazine and wider, detailed instructions on how to carry out a particular task, and creative writing in a number of genres – historical, fantasy, detective, romantic, humour, science fiction and so on.

- ✍ Try to make available examples of texts by professional writers of the genre that your child is using for a particular piece of writing. This 'modelling' is an important part of the process. The aim is to see successful examples of the genre rather than to use them to copy styles.

- ✍ Organize visits to a wide variety of locations to provide raw material for the senses to promote future writing.

- ✍ Provide a notebook so that your child can jot down ideas whenever they come to mind.

- ✍ Encourage your able and talented child to experiment with writing and to play about with the boundaries of a genre. Set up a series of interesting challenges – writing a prequel or sequel to an existing story, putting together a script for a group of puppets or for a toy theatre, writing a new version of a traditional story. This may well play to the singular sense of humour that many able children have.

- ✍ Have available sets of Magnetic Poetry, available from many bookshops, and a suitable board. A larger area can be created by painting a surface with magnetic paint. Let your child experiment with the available words.

- ✍ Obtain copies of the *Mini Saga* books published by Sutton Publishing. These are based upon the *Daily Telegraph* competitions, where participants have to write a story with a beginning, middle and an end in exactly 50 words. The title is outside that 50 but must not be more than 15 words long. Get your child to have a go. Run a competition for family and friends or enter the next *Daily Telegraph* competition. To do this, your child has to weigh every word.

- ✍ Promote creativity in your child's writing by supplying some initial stimuli. An outstanding way is to look at *The Mysteries of Harris Burdick* by Chris Van Allsburg. As well as the book version there is a portfolio edition made up of posters. Get your child to write a story based upon one of the mysteries. To help stimulate the imagination, there is an intriguing black-and-white drawing, the title and one provocative line of information. You and your child can also visit *The Mysteries of Harris Burdick* website to share stories and interpretations (*www.hmco.com/vanallsburg*). Magic awaits! Try reversing the process by getting your child to find unusual pictures and to add a suitable title and one-liner.

Extend the connection between pictures and creative writing by getting a copy of Quentin Blake's *Tell Me a Picture*. The author has chosen 26 paintings and illustrations from children's books. Typical Quentin Blake characters ask pointed questions. Your child is invited to tell a story or write a poem based upon the painting or illustration. The book followed an exhibition at the National Gallery in London. There is also a website (*www.nationalgallery.org.uk*).

Suggest that your able child enters the Foyle Young Poets of the Year award. This is a joint venture between The Poetry Society and The Foyle Foundation. The scheme is aimed at the 11–18 years' age group. Details can be obtained from The Education Department, The Poetry Society, 22 Betterton Street, London WC2H 9BX (telephone 020 7420 9894, email *education@poetrysociety.org.uk*, website *www.poetrysociety.org.uk*). An anthology of young poets' work is published yearly. Membership of the society includes receiving a Young Writer's Pack.

# READING

Establish reading habits as a family. Parents who read and obviously appreciate books are much more likely to encourage their children to read. If possible, create particular times when it is the norm to read. You may wish to read Aidan Chambers' *The Reading Environment* which is subtitled *How Adults Help Children Enjoy Books*.

Encourage your able child to meet others who share a love of literature. This might be achieved through enrichment courses or a reading group. It is always a great pleasure to share enthusiasms.

Make time to discuss books with your child – which is known as conferencing. Try to obtain a copy of *Tell Me: Children, Reading and Talk* by Aidan Chambers. Written by an acknowledged expert, the book provides 'a repertoire of questions that assist readers in speaking about their reading. *Tell Me* is about helping children to talk well about books they have read. And not only talk well but listen well.' Many teachers have a copy of the book but the 'enabling adult' could equally well be a parent. Very practical techniques are described including 'The Three Sharings' – sharing enthusiasms, sharing puzzles (that is, difficulties), sharing connections (that is, discovering patterns).

Obtain copies of books about children's authors; able children are often curious about what is in the mind of writers. *Talking Books: Children's Authors Talk about the Craft, Creativity and Process of Writing*, by James Carter, is a collection of interviews with Brian Moses, Benjamin Zephaniah, Ian Beck, Neil Ardley, Terry Deary, Helen Cresswell, Gillian Cross, Bertie Doherty, Alan Durant, Philip Pullman, Celia Rees, Norman Silver and Jacqueline Wilson. At the end of the book there is also a useful miscellany of information on children's books.

- Avoid pressing your able child to be always reading a book of acknowledged difficulty and quality. Clearly you will want them to make contact with the best but children, as well as adults, sometimes relax with trivial material.

- Explore the rich resources of Booktrust, Book House, 45 East Hill, London SW18 2QZ (telephone 020 8516 2981/8516 2977, email *Deborah@booktrust.org.uk*, website *www.booktrusted.com* and *www.booktrust.org.uk*). There is a free Parents' Pack containing general advice on obtaining and selecting books, together with specific guidance on the relevant age range and age-targeted booklists. *Booktrusted News* is a quarterly magazine featuring news and views on various aspects of the children's book world. Each issue concentrates on a particular theme and contains a related pull-out booklist. Also included are author and illustrator profiles, information about book prizes, reviews of new titles, from baby books to teenage reads, and a variety of articles about children's books and reading. *Best Book Guide* is the new name for *100 Best Books* (back issues of which are still available), which has been expanded to include even more reviews. The *Guide* is Booktrust's independent annual pick of the best in children's paperback fiction published in the previous calendar year. It is designed to help parents, teachers, librarians, booksellers and anyone interested in children's reading to select books for children from babies to teenagers. Printed in full colour, each book featured has a short review, easy colour coding to indicate reading age and interest level, plus some bibliographical information for easy ordering at bookshops and libraries. Booktrust also has a good selection of posters, stickers and bookmarks available.

- Be aware of the dangers of your child reading a book ahead of his or her social and emotional development; able readers have the skills to read a book technically well ahead of their chronological age. This works well unless the book also has a social and emotional setting beyond the child's age, such as experience of adolescence. In cases such as this, the child loses much of the meaning as their life experience lags behind technical ability.

- Make bookcases an important part of the furniture to stress the central role of reading. If the purchase of many books is not financially viable, organize regular trips to the local library.

- Appreciate that reading can involve a variety of materials. Some boys prefer non-fiction. Poetry is an important area that can be neglected.

- Be careful about relying too much on your own childhood reading when recommending books to your able child. Some of what was regarded as good is still very worthwhile, while some has dated badly. In any case, too much reliance upon what you read might mean that your child misses out on what is currently in print. Children's literature has never been stronger; a treasure chest of riches is now available. Indeed, many would claim that some of the best titles generally today are from children's authors. If you are not familiar with the new array of talent, take one or more of the following routes – look

at information from Booktrust (details above), acquire guides prepared by the large book chains, such as Waterstone's, take advice from the bookshelves of large shops (staff make recommendations through a card system), take advice from the local library expert on children's literature, look at the recommended reading list by the author that follows this section of the parents' and carers' guide.

- Explore youth membership (ages 11–18 years) of The Poetry Society (contact details given in the writing section above) that produces a quarterly review and newsletter as well as books and materials for teachers and students.

- Keep an eye on developments at the Centre for the Children's Book, which was set up in 1996 to 'place children and their books at the heart of our national culture'. Past exhibitions there have been very popular. The Centre is to change its name to Seven Stories and is in the process of moving offices: 'When complete, exhibitions will fill the galleries and visitors of all ages will have the chance to explore the world of children's books. You'll be able to meet writers and artists, have a break in our café and browse in our superb children's bookshop. At the heart of the Centre will be an important collection of the work of modern writers and illustrators for children, more than 100 of whom have pledged work' (keep in touch via email, *info@childrensbook.org.uk*, website, *www.childrensbook.org.uk*).

- When visiting bookshops and libraries, take time in selecting books and be open to the views of your able child. Be prepared to experiment with unusual and interesting books to extend the range of reading.

# GEOGRAPHY

 Organize family visits to see natural features, such as cliffs, rivers and limestone areas, as well as to features of a man-made environment, for instance, settlement patterns. Encourage questioning about what is seen: 'How did it get like this?' or 'How and why is it changing?' Also visit factories, planning departments, power stations, water authorities and so on.

 Make contact with the Geographical Association, 160 Solly Street, Sheffield S1 4BF (telephone 0114 296 0088, email *ga@geography.org.uk*, website *www.geography.org.uk*). There are two resources catalogues: one for early years and primary and the other for secondary and beyond. Comprehensive descriptions can be found online at *www.geographyshop.org.uk*, where you can also order resources electronically. Although primarily aimed at teachers, the materials will be of interest to the parents and carers of able children. Examples from the early years and primary catalogue are *Geography Through Play* by Angela M. Milner, encouraging the use of indoor and outdoor play as an approach to geographical learning, and *Placing Places* by Simon Catling – 250 ways to help children build up a mental map of the Earth, plus a rationale for locational knowledge. Among the resources in the secondary and beyond catalogue are *The Geographer's Guide to the Internet* by Karl Donert (self-explanatory), *World Puzzle Book* by Andrew Dalwood (a variety of geography puzzles to make the subject more lively and help children learn in an enjoyable way) and *Atlas-Wise: Ideas and Themes for Atlas Work* by Stephen Scoffham (practical activities involving atlases and world maps).

There are two main events that the Geographical Association holds specifically for children. The first, 'Worldwide Quiz', seeks to bring schools and pupils together in an enjoyable, face-to-face, out-of-school activity designed to promote pupils' interest in geography and its popularity in the schools. Local rounds take place between October and January with the winner of each local round going through to the regional final sponsored by the Field Studies Council. The second, 'Geography Action Week', is usually

held in October. The Geographical Association provides a themed poster with activities to follow. Check with your school about entering a team for the 'Worldwide Quiz' or taking part in 'Geography Action Week'.

- Find time to discuss with your able child the many issues and contrasting points of view involved in geography such as land use, global warming, water shortages, the transport system, nuclear energy and pollution.

- An enjoyable and interesting book is *Where in the World Am I?*, edited by Simon Melhuish. With the help of ten clues, in an order of decreasing difficulty, you have to work out which city, country or place is being described. See how many your able child can identify, then get your child to write some new examples. The order of the clues is the key requirement.

- The magazine *National Geographic* can be obtained by subscription (membership 1-800-647-5463, website *www.nationalgeographic.com/ngm*) available direct or from outlets such as WH Smith. There are substantial features, lavishly illustrated with stunning photographs.

- Try to arrange work experience with organizations such as the Environment Agency, local planning departments and transport companies who deal with geographically based issues, when your child is the appropriate age.

- Ask your child to plan a treasure hunt for pedestrians or cyclists, where all the clues have a geographical basis.

- Look to develop your child's geographical vocabulary. For primary-age children there is *The Questions Dictionary of Geography and the Environment* by Joy Palmer. The book introduces children to key geographical vocabulary and specialist terms. It is available from Questions Publishing Company, Leonard House, 321 Bradford Street, Digbeth, Birmingham B5 6ET (telephone 0121 666 7878, email *sales@questpub.co.uk*, website *www.education-quest.com*). Try playing the author's 'Generating Geographical Glossary'. The child has to define a geographical term by using only words that alliterate with it. An example would be: 'Earthquake: epicentre, earthshaking, energy, endemic'.

- Explore the world of orienteering. This is the sport of making one's way quickly across difficult country with the help of a map and compass. Consider events such as 'Ten Tors' where teams of youngsters make their way across Dartmoor following instructions and using a compass.

- Provide a sketchbook for your able child to record the main geographical feature of any location being visited. Stress that you do not have to be a great artist to be able to record what is seen in simple terms. Labels can also be added. This technique encourages the child to analyse a view for its geographical content. It also provides a visual record for use in the future. 'Field sketching', as it is known, was one of several methods recommended by the Geographical Association for its 'Geography Action Week' 2003.

⊕ Encourage your able child to write a 'Geographical Tangled Tale'. The object is to write a short story that flows and makes sense but one that contains, say, 20 items of geographical vocabulary. This activity plays upon the fact that many words have a general meaning as well as a specific geographical meaning. Examples of such words are meander, source and stack.

⊕ Look to develop the skill of 'visual literacy' in your able child through interpreting maps, graphs, diagrams, aerial photographs and satellite images. Get your child to plan a route for a real or imaginary journey. Ordnance Survey produces a set of 'Map Symbol Flashcards' for young children. They are available from the Geographical Association (contact details above). Ask older children to create a game using the map symbol cards. Satellite postcards can also be purchased from the Geographical Association. Ask your child to study suitable photographs, old and new, and get as much information as possible from the visual evidence on view through questions such as 'Where is this likely to be?', 'Who are the people?', 'When was the photograph taken?', 'Is the area rich or poor?', 'What activity is shown?', 'What might this place be like in 20 years' time?', and 'How does the photograph inform you about the climate of the location shown?'. 'Reading photographs' is one of a number of thinking skills advocated by David Leat of the University of Newcastle and the 'Thinking Through Geography' team in the north-east of England.

⊕ Organize family walks, rambles or hikes, depending upon the physical capacity of the members. Encourage your child to use a map of the area so that he or she can relate the two-dimensional conventions of the paper to the three-dimensional realities of the landscape.

⊕ Make available materials so that your able child can construct three-dimensional models of a landscape.

⊕ Keep a watch on television schedules for suitable programmes. Natural history programmes, such as those presented by David Attenborough, have a strong geographical background. Travel series abound and satellite channels such as National Geographic, Discovery, UK Horizons and Animal Planet have programmes of interest.

⊕ Obtain holiday brochures from travel agents and then ask your able child to rewrite one with a view to attract tourists particularly interested in geography and the environment.

⊕ Explore the possibilities of children's literature. In many novels and poems there is an insight into other people's lives and places far away from home. Different viewpoints are presented through fictional situations that mirror real life. Many stories contain maps of real or fictional places and characters make journeys through different lands. The Geographical Association (contact details above) has a number of relevant titles. The 'Barnaby Bear' collection of resources offers an innovative approach to exploring the wider world with young children. Further 'Barnaby Bear' resources are available from the BBC (*www.bbc.co.uk/schools/barnabybear*). *Place In Story-time* by Heather Norris Nicholson

looks to using story to develop children's geographical understanding at primary-school age through a sense of place. *The Storylink* series, by Iain Dryden and Ralph Hare, links stories to studying geography for junior-age children. One project concerns Llandudno in Wales, another Kochi in southern India.

- Develop your child's understanding of the links between climate, topography and human activity. Ask your able child to create a new island or country large enough to have contrasting areas. The various components must make sense geographically. A map should be drawn, accompanied by short, written extracts on the climate, agriculture, landscape, industry, economy, people and indigenous animals. To stimulate the imagination, try to get a look at Paul Warren's magical book *Caleb Beldragon's Chronicle of the Three Counties*.

- Involve your child in any opportunity that arises in your locality involving a public enquiry, such as a proposed bypass or a major planning application for changed use of land.

- Ask your child to re-plan the village, town or city where you live so that a beneficial use is made of local features. A discussion of the term 'beneficial use' would, in itself, be valuable.

- Use maps of Britain for fun purposes. It is amazing how poor the knowledge of even able children is about the position of places in their own country. Try two activities devised by the author. In 'The Geography Person' children build up a human being from place names such as Chester, Northumberland, Exmouth and Aberystwyth. They are encouraged to use their sense of humour by using puns and word play, but within the bounds of decency! 'The People of Britain' can be played on journeys or at home. Children are asked to place groups of people in appropriate places – 'The clean people of Bath', 'The horse riders of Canterbury', 'The auditors of Stockport' and 'The cautious people of Watchet'. Great fun!

- Get your child to set a crossword where all the clues and answers have a geographical basis.

- Have a look at the 'Geography in Evidence' catalogue by TTS, Nunn Brook Road, Huthwaite, Sutton-in-Ashfield, Nottinghamshire NG17 2HU (telephone 0800 318686, email *sales@tts-group.co.uk*, website *www.tts-group.co.uk*). There are maps, atlases, jigsaws, CD-ROMs, globes and artefacts. A couple of eye-catching items are the book *If the World Were a Village* that enables the reader to conceptualize the whole world as if it were a single village inhabited by only 100 people, and a wooden structure to create your own riverbank called 'Riverslide'. It can be filled with natural or man-made materials and water can then be run through to show how river erosion occurs.

- Help your able child to set up a weather station at home. Encourage the regular recording of data and discussion about interpretation, meaning and consequences.

# HISTORY

- Look for opportunities to work with primary sources – census returns, documents, diaries, letters and so on. One particular activity that promotes such use is tracing the family history – bookshops sell beginner's guides on how to do this. The county Records Office is a likely destination.

- Join the local History Society for a programme of talks and other activities.

- Subscribe to, or borrow copies of, magazines such as *History Today* and *BBC History*. They are readily available at WH Smith and other outlets.

- Encourage the use of more advanced texts than the standard textbook for topics that your able and talented child is covering at school. Work with the school to get copies or a list of suitable titles. See what is available at your local library. Able children require greater variety and complexity to extend their understanding and appreciation.

- Play 'History What If?'. Get your child to speculate on what would have happened if a key event had gone differently. The situations can be fitted to areas of work being studied at school. 'What would have happened if the plot to assassinate Julius Caesar had been foiled?' 'What would have happened if Hitler had carried out a successful invasion of Britain?' The speculation should be informed by existing knowledge. In the case of the latter example, certain events would definitely have taken place – arresting leaders and known opponents, the banning of trade unions, changes in the education system, the strict control of the press, to name a few. But would Britain have had comparatively lenient treatment, like Denmark, or harsh treatment, like Poland? Knowledge of Hitler's attitude to racial groups would inform the speculation.

- Encourage your able child to meet others of like mind and interest. This may be through the History Club at school or at enrichment courses run by the LEA, the National Association for Gifted Children or private groups.

- Explore the role of poetry in history. Ask your child to explain the meaning behind poems like 'The Mask of Anarchy' by Percy Bysshe Shelley. Secure a copy of the wonderfully entertaining *A Rhyming History of Britain* by James Muirden. Get your child to write something in the same style about one particular event or person.

- Organize visits to museums, archaeological sites, battle sites, castles, old houses and so on. Ask such pertinent questions as about the lie of the land, the positioning of a defence point, the height and shape of windows, or the meaning of a feature. Go beyond simple observation to higher-order thinking and understanding – why has it been designed like that? There are also places to explore where children can experience, briefly, life at other times by dressing up in period costume or sampling a schoolday back in the past. Libraries and Tourist Information Centres (TICs) carry details about the availability of such places in particular localities.

- Access the very large number of history programmes being broadcast on television. More than ever before are available on the normal terrestrial channels. Also be aware of the richness available through the UKTV History channel available on satellite.

- Ask your able child to make a considered evaluation, in historical terms, of the accuracy of popular television dramatizations such as that on Henry VIII, broadcast in 2003. Is the accompanying publicity fair or is it deliberately sensationalized to expand the viewing audience?

- Attend talks by professional historians, especially when part of the presentation concerns their skills and working methods.

- Look to your able child entering history-based competitions. A number of prizes are offered annually, at primary, secondary and post-16 levels, by the Young Historian Project, 36 Heritage Court, Lichfield, Staffordshire WS14 9ST (website *www.harappa.com/teach/YHistcomp.htm*). The organizer, Dr Trevor James, can be contacted on 01543 301097. Discussion with your child's school is advisable as the purpose of the prizes is to encourage classroom history. However, all the challenges can be used as activities beyond the normal classroom. One can only applaud the motto of the organization – 'We wish to celebrate excellence'.

- Make quality time available to debate historical issues with your able child so that he or she can develop and demonstrate ideas.

- Place your child in the shoes of somebody in history with a problem to solve. Stress that any proposed solutions must fit the resources and knowledge of the time. An example would be William Mompesson, the rector of the village of Eyam, faced with an outbreak of plague in 1665.

- Look at the historical benefits, and increased knowledge and understanding to come from your able child collecting old postcards or stamps.

- Encourage the reading of novels that have a strong historical content. Henrietta Branford's *Fire, Bed and Bone* tells the story of the Peasants' Revolt through the eyes of a dog. *The Alchymist's Cat* by Robin Jarvis has seventeenth-century London as its setting and includes alchemy and plague among its subjects. Award-winning author Theresa Breslin deals with the Western Front during the First World War in *Remembrance*. The former glories of the steel industry are central to Theresa Tomlinson's *Meet Me by the Steelmen*. Author Caroline Lawrence studied Classical Archaeology at Cambridge. Her Roman Mysteries series, published by Orion, follows the exploits of Flavia Gemina, a Roman sea captain's daughter, and her three friends Jonathan, the Jewish boy next door, Nubia the African slave-girl and Lupus, the mute beggar boy. Aristo's Scroll, at the end of each book, explains the words and names. Titles so far include *The Thieves of Ostia, The Secrets of Vesuvius, The Pirates of Pompeii, Assassins of Rome, The Dolphins of Laurentum* and *The Twelve Tasks of Flavia Gemina*. Hans Magnus Enzensberger is one of Germany's most eminent authors. His unusual book *Where Were You Robert?* has been translated into 13 languages and is an international bestseller. Robert finds himself adrift in history as a result of staring into a film or TV screen or a painting. His experiences take him into other times and places, farther and farther away from his home and his own time. Librarians are a good source of information on children's books with good historical content.

- Explore the fascinating world of archaeology. There are a growing number of television programmes, such as *Time Team* and *Two Men in a Trench*. Books accompany the series. Contact the Young Archaeologists' Club at Council for British Archaeology, Bowes Morrell House, 111 Walmgate, York YO1 9WA (telephone 01904 671417, website *www.britarch.ac.uk/yac*). Please note that there is a planned change of address in the future but the website will remain the same. Membership of the Young Archaeologists' Club, open to 8–16 year olds, offers four magazines a year, competitions, discounted entry to museums and archaeological centres and information about the 70 local branches (where children get hands-on experience, doing anything from excavation to experimental archaeology and designing museum activities), archaeological holidays, National Archaeology Days and the Young Archaeologist of the Year Award. An interesting spin-off is for your child to get involved as a metal detectorist. Check for the existence of a local group. Archaeologists used to dislike the activities of such groups but attitudes have changed, there is a code of practice and detectorists have made important finds.

- Take a look at the world of war games, unless you have moral objections. Boys, in particular, are fascinated by using the sets of figures available. Follow the television programme *Time Commander* in which members of the public re-fight old battles with computer simulation, as historians comment upon their plans.

- Obtain copies of the Horrible Histories series. They play to the particular sense of humour possessed by many able children.

- Take a look at the catalogue of resources, *History In Evidence*, produced by TTS, Nunn Brook Road, Huthwaite, Sutton-in-Ashfield, Nottinghamshire NG17 2HU (telephone 0800 318686, email *sales@tts-group.co.uk*, website *www.tts-group.co.uk*). Items include books, maps, artefacts, posters, kits, videos, CD-ROMs, coins, wall charts, costumes and games.

- Strengthen the higher-order thinking skills of analysis, synthesis and evaluation in your able child by using materials concerned with detective work. Lagoon publishes short detective case books. The author includes many detective materials in his resource books for able and talented children, published by Network Educational Press.

- See if codes fascinate your able child. Their abstract quality is very suitable for high ability. Julius Caesar developed a code; the Spartans developed one based on their uniform's staff; Mary, Queen of Scots died because her poor code was broken by Elizabeth's advisers; the Second World War was shortened by the cracking of the German Enigma code. A wonderful text to explore is Simon Singh's *The Code Book: The Secret History of Codes and Code-breaking*.

- Construct various timelines – family, locality, country, continent, global, favourite football club, whatever! This helps the appreciation of chronology in your able child. Certain publications use this approach. *A Street Through Time* by Dr Anne Millard and Steve Noon traces one particular street through 12,000 years during 14 key periods in history. It is beautifully illustrated.

- Contact the British Museum, London, WC1B 3DG (website *www.british-museum.ac.uk*), to find out about its considerable services that offer a range of learning experiences for everyone, whatever the age or level of interest. 'Children's COMPASS' allows you to browse hundreds of incredible objects online. You can also play games, print out activities, send in work to the Notice board or pose questions to 'Ask the Expert'.

- Investigate the resources catalogue produced by English Heritage Education, Freepost 22 (WD 214), London W1E 7EZ (telephone customer services 0870 333 1181, email *education@english-heritage.org.uk*, website *www.english-heritage.org.uk/education*). There are books, videos, posters, photographs and CD-ROMs. Although primarily aimed at teachers, the majority of the resources could be used by parents with their children and some materials can now be downloaded from the website. The *Heritage Learning* magazine, published three times a year, is produced for schools but it is available free to all those interested in the educational use of the historic environment. There are many interesting features. For instance, in the autumn 2003 edition there was a feature showing how to 'make your own chain mail' plus advance details of a major event on the History channel, The Family History Project looking for people 'to present the stories that bring the names on their family trees to life – stories of the famous, infamous and notorious as well as stories of emigration, interesting professions and personal achievement' (*www.thefamilyhistoryproject.co.uk*).

# MATHEMATICS

 Try to work in partnership with your able child's school so that there is no overlap and repetition of work undertaken. However, if it proves difficult to secure appropriate resources, look to obtaining challenging materials, of a non-standard type, at home. Some publications are aimed at teachers and parents. A good example is the series of *Maths Challenge* books (*One*, *Two* and *Three*) edited by Tony Gardiner and published by Oxford University Press (customer services telephone 01536 741068). They are aimed to 'stretch able students in lower secondary schools' but able junior-age pupils would get benefit as well. Each book has challenges, comments and solutions plus a glossary.

Encourage the use of a maths dictionary, as mathematical vocabulary is an important area within curriculum guidelines. Many types are available, but one with a particular format is *Mathematics: A Dictionary of How to Do It* by Julie Gibbon and published by Claire Publications, Unit 8, Tey Brook Craft Centre, Great Tey, Colchester, Essex CO6 1JE. It aims to help parents, carers and pupils by providing a handy reference book. Able children might like to supplement such a text with entries of their own. Oxford Paperbacks publish a more advanced version: Christopher Clapham's *Concise Dictionary of Mathematics*.

Avoid pushing your child to do 'more of the same'. Look instead for things that are different and that give both a challenge and enjoyment.

Encourage experimental thinking with provocative questions such as: 'What if the numbers were changed?', 'What if we rotate it?', 'What if we consider this in three dimensions rather than two?'

On family outings and holidays, get your able child to put on 'mathematical glasses' to appreciate the maths all around us. Mazes are very mathematical; look at castles for their trajectory, and so on.

Build up a collection of individual books for interest or borrow copies from the library. Look for fascinating material that makes maths 'live'. Titles might include: *The Number Devil* by Hans Magnus Enzensberger; *The Joy of Pi* by David Blatner; *Four Colours Suffice: How the Map Problem was Solved* by Robin Wilson; and *Introducing Mathematics* by Ziauddin Sardar, Jerry Ravetz and Borin Van Loon. Advanced students would enjoy the books of Professor Ian Stewart, such as *The Magical Maze: Seeing the World through Mathematical Eyes* and *Game, Set and Math: Enigmas and Conundrums*.

Explore the internet for mathematical problems and investigations. A particularly good source is the NRICH On-line Maths Club at *www.nrich.maths.org.uk*

Encourage participation in mathematical quizzes: events such as treasure hunts, mathematical mastermind, tournaments and regional and national maths' competitions. The United Kingdom Mathematics Trust (UKMT) runs challenges annually. The Junior Challenge is aimed at the top 35 per cent of pupils nationwide in Years 7 and 8 and the Intermediate is for pupils in Years 9–11. The Senior Challenge is aimed at all pupils below Year 13 who are studying maths at AS or A-level standard. Top scorers from all the challenges are invited to take part in a 'follow-on' round. Parents cannot enter children individually; this must take place via the school. However, UKMT has produced booklets containing the last five years' Maths Challenges for the Junior and Intermediate competitions and the last four years for the Senior competition. Details can be obtained from UKMT, School of Mathematics, University of Leeds, Leeds LS2 9JT (telephone 0113 343 2339, email *enquiry@ukmt.org.uk*, website *www.ukmt.org.uk*).

Run a family, or wider, event in which everybody has to write a poem with a mathematical theme. Theoni Pappas writes poems to be performed by two voices in *Math Talk: Mathematical Ideas in Poems for Two Voices*.

Involve your mathematically able child in enrichment sessions run by NAGC or LEAs, or in masterclasses run by organizations such as the Royal Institution (*www.rigb.org*). Masterclasses are supported by the Gabbitas, Truman and Thring Educational Trust (*www.masterclasses.co.uk*).

Play games, as a family, that have a mathematical content of some sort. The domino game Fives and Threes is a good example. *Strategy Games File* by Reg Sheppard and John Wilkinson is a collection of 50 games and puzzles to stimulate mathematical thinking. 'The games and puzzles in this collection require children to look for patterns and relationships while encouraging the development of ideas about number, space, tessellations, shapes, boundaries and networks. Players are encouraged to communicate their findings and to express them precisely in symbols.' The book is published by Tarquin Publications, Stradbroke, Diss, Norfolk IP21 5JP (telephone 01379 384218, website *www.tarquin-books.demon.co.uk*). It would be worthwhile securing a copy of their catalogue as there is a strong mathematical representation within the materials on offer, such as *The Tessellations File* by Chris de Cordova, *Pascal's Triangle* by Tony

Colledge, *The Number File* by Adrian Jenkins and *Mathematical Treasure-Hunts* by Vivien Lucas.

Access the world-class tests for 9–13 year olds at *www.worldclassarena.org*

Contact The Mathematical Association, 259 London Road, Leicester LE2 3BE (telephone 0116 221 0013, email *office@m-a.org.uk*, website *www.m-a.org.uk*). Resources include books, stickers, posters and postcards, as well as two journals for pupils: *Symmetry Plus +* and *Mathematical Pie*.

Have available a range of puzzles to challenge and entertain. General puzzle books have maths problems among other areas. MENSA includes number puzzles within its publications which are readily available via normal bookshops. A series of new editions from MENSA include *MENSA Number Puzzles for Kids*. There are six levels of difficulty: 'Easy Does It'; 'Getting Harder'; 'Fiendish Figures'; 'Mind Numbing'; 'Aaargh!'; and 'Super Genius'. Dover Publications is an American company that has a bookshop in London. In the catalogue are maths puzzle books including those from legendary figures such as H. E. Dudeney and Sam Lloyd. Martin Gardner is another renowned figure and he is published by Dover and by Penguin Books. Brian Bolt has a number of excellent books published by Cambridge University Press. They cover many different aspects of maths and they are presented in the form of problems and puzzles: *The Amazing Mathematical Amusement Arcade*; *Mathematical Funfair*; *Mathematical Cavalcade*; *A Mathematical Pandora's Box*; and *Mathematical Jamboree*. The Happy Puzzle Company (PO Box 24041, London NW4 2ZN, website *www.happypuzzle.co.uk*) has a mail-order catalogue containing a wide range of products. Tantrix is particularly good for visual perception and sequencing but, be warned, it is totally addictive! A new game, Set!, looks very interesting, with its emphasis upon visual perception and strategic planning.

Have a look at the resources produced by ATM (the Association of Teachers of Mathematics), 7 Shaftesbury Street, Derby DE23 8YB (telephone 01332 346599, email *admin@atm.org.uk*, website *www.atm.org.uk*). There are activity books, playing cards, discussion books, games, posters, software and postcards. A particular favourite of the author is The Fourbidden Card Game where children try to define a mathematical term without using four, forbidden words – the ones, of course, that you most want to use. Get your mathematically able child to design more of his or her own.

Encourage logical thinking through 'related activities', as we might call them. Matrix puzzles put an emphasis upon logical thinking and handling data. Books of them are available from WH Smith and other outlets. WH Smith also stock Tsunami Puzzles, which originated in Japan. Sets of numbers vertically and horizontally are cross-referenced to indicate which squares can be blocked in. Eventually a picture emerges. They can also be received by subscription from British European Associated Publisher Limited, Stonecroft, 69 Station Road, Redhill, Surrey RH1 1EY.

■ Get your mathematically able child to write an article for a mathematical magazine or to write a story in which as many maths terms as possible are included in disguised form, such as parallel, average, frequency and so on.

■ Contact SMILE Mathematics, Isaac Newton Centre, 108A Lancaster Road, London W11 1QS (telephone 020 7598 4841, email *info@smilemathematics.co.uk*, website *www.smilemathematics.co.uk*) to get a copy of their resources, including software. Sets of playing cards, fraction, decimal, equivalence and number, could be used for many games. Let your mathematically able child create new games using the cards.

# MODERN FOREIGN LANGUAGES

The phrase 'target language' indicates the particular language or languages that your child has high ability in, whether it be French, Spanish, German, Italian, Portuguese, Russian or whatever.

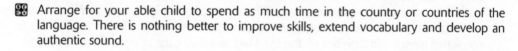

▣ Arrange for your able child to spend as much time in the country or countries of the language. There is nothing better to improve skills, extend vocabulary and develop an authentic sound.

▣ Arrange for your able child to read a newspaper in the target language on a regular basis.

▣ Have readily available a set of Magnetic Poetry. There are versions in Italian, French, Spanish and so on. A number of shops, including Waterstone's, sell them. Each set contains some 500 pieces. A metallic surface or special board is needed. You can provide a larger area by covering a suitable space with 'attract-a-magnet paint'. This was the brainchild of World's Greatest Minds Ltd, 3 Palace Yard Mews, Bath BA1 2NH. It is available in the resource catalogue of The Happy Puzzle Company (telephone 0800 376 3728, website *www.happypuzzle.co.uk*).

▣ Try to organize work experience at a company that has strong connections with the desired country, when your child is the appropriate age.

▣ Use interesting picture books, with no words, as the stimulus for a piece of writing. As there is no text, the pictures can be interpreted at any level of sophistication and in any language. Books such as *Clown* by Quentin Blake are very suitable.

- Find opportunities for your able child to work with other children of a similar ability and like mind. This may be achieved through enrichment sessions run by LEAs (some run short, intensive courses) or private groups. This contact can be highly beneficial.

- Contact local universities to see what they are able to offer. This might involve advanced days in a language such as German or sampler days in languages such as Japanese, or a session on linguistics – how languages are constructed.

- Explore what facilities, outside normal lessons, are available at school. This might be drop-in lunchtime sessions, an after-school languages club or extra time with one of the language assistants.

- Take a look at the resources provided by European Schoolbooks Limited, The Runnings, Cheltenham GL51 9PQ (telephone 01242 245252, email *direct@esb.co.uk*, website *www.eurobooks.co.uk*). There is an extensive catalogue of French, German, Italian and Spanish resources, including readers, music, video cassettes, games and language practice. The age range covered is from pre-school to 15. You can place orders online, by phone, fax, post or email. If convenient, visit the European Bookshop, 5 Warwick Street, London W1B 5LU.

- Subscribe to a language magazine. ELI Magazines have been a familiar medium for language learning worldwide for more than 20 years. French, German, Spanish, Italian and Russian magazines are available, as well as Latin and English. They are graded for several levels: primary beginners; secondary beginners; lower intermediate; intermediate; upper intermediate; and advanced. All subscriptions comprise six issues. Different magazines offer country-specific articles, illustrations, comic-strips, songs, rhymes, posters, word games, articles from foreign newspapers and collectables. There are also more interactive games and activities on the ELI Magazines' website at *www.elimagazines.com*. The magazines themselves can be ordered from European Schoolbooks Limited (contact details above).

- Get involved in twinning activities if there is a suitable opportunity in your locality.

- Have available a really good dictionary. Get your child to explore its wealth. Nominate a particular letter and then ask your child to put together a picture made up of objects starting with that letter in the target language. This can be done as a drawing to use art skills, a collage by cutting up old magazines or by putting together items from computer graphic packages, using ICT skills. Also advise that 'abstract' words can be portrayed, such as the horizon or an emotion.

- Play games such as Scrabble and Lexicon but in the target language. Decide with your child whether the scoring system needs to be changed or the frequency of letters can be changed by combining sets, to take account of differences in the use of particular letters in other languages. That discussion itself would be most instructive.

Build up a collection of novels and poetry in the target language, or borrow copies. Get advice from your able child's school on suitable titles to take him or her forward.

Acquire a good book of word games in English such as Tony Augarde's *The Oxford Guide to Word Games*. Ask your able and talented child to find games that are interesting and then to decide whether they will work in the target language. For those games that are suitable, see if the child can create examples in the required language. Many work well and are very entertaining.

Get your child to set a crossword where the answers are in the target language. The clues can be in English or in the required language to make the challenge much more difficult.

Through a recognized organization, involve your child in a pen-pal scheme with the country required. Contact can now be made by email.

Organize as much contact as possible with family members and friends who speak the target language, native speakers and visiting adults.

# MUSIC

Music is regarded as one of the most obvious examples of the need for support by parents and carers to achieve success by the children.

Be aware that skills and enthusiasm shown by younger children do not always continue as the children get older. Meaningful and long-term commitment is more easily recognized in early adolescence. Pressurizing children who no longer want to devote much of their time to music may be counterproductive. However, there is a vital need to start musical activity early in life.

Obtain the relevant information about opportunities in your town, city or county. This may come in the format of a parents' and carers' information booklet and/or a website.

Before deciding on a particular instrument, get expert advice. Some authorities organize preparatory lessons for beginners that act as taster sessions and aim to ensure 'instrument compatibility'.

If possible, purchase the appropriate instrument. Going through an educational authority can reduce costs by not having to pay VAT. If not, look to hire an instrument from your local authority or music shop.

Explore the possibility of financial assistance and the availability of scholarships and awards, either from the local area or trust funds and charities. Public libraries often have this information.

- Provide suitable rehearsal space and time. Establish a regular practice routine rather than allowing erratic bursts of activity. Talk to your child about what has happened in lessons and then encourage meaningful practice to follow them. If there is a practice record book, take the opportunity to record your comments.

- Establish regular communication with the specialist teacher and other experts. Taking note of the advice of professionals is important to development. Discussions with other able students are also to be encouraged.

- Organize visits to concerts, recitals and shows. Help the child to broaden musical horizons by dipping into a wide variety of styles. If possible, provide a range of CDs to give a rich listening experience.

- Support attendance at a range of regular extra-curricular activities – concert orchestra, jazz orchestra, string ensemble, percussion group, choir and so on. Activities are often available at local music centres. Look out for special teaching weeks, performance weeks, short courses, weekend gatherings and masterclasses. Take any opportunity for your child to play alongside professional musicians.

- Encourage opportunities to measure your child's musical progress by entering external instrumental examinations, festivals and competitions. However, do not make grade attainment too dominating a goal. This can be counterproductive. Some authorities issue bronze, silver and gold awards to mark outstanding musical achievement.

- Look to the needs of a variety of musical talents. Composition, for instance, needs substantial blocks of time, as well as competence in keyboard and computer skills. Many strands of musical activity are equally worthwhile. Experimentation is to be encouraged. Unusual routes can be most beneficial.

- Be prepared to display patience and understanding over the long-term development because of the nature of your child's musical ability. Social skills, tolerance and self-confidence are parts of this development, as well as technical skills. There will inevitably be highs and lows. Your child needs help to learn from both successes and difficulties.

- Keep an eye on the radio and television schedules. Radio 3 has a wealth of performances. The Artsworld channel, on digital television, has a strong musical content.

- Encourage your able child to use a specialist dictionary. *The Questions Dictionary of Music* by Karen Thornton is aimed at junior and lower secondary children. It can be ordered on 0121 666 7878, or by email *sales@questpub.co.uk*. Ask your able child to research and add extra terms. Oxford Paperbacks publish the *Concise Oxford Dictionary of Music* by Nigel Kennedy.

# PE, SPORT AND DANCE

This is a very special area where parents and carers can become overambitious if they are not careful. Advice in this section contains some important 'don'ts' as well as some important 'dos'.

Encourage an attitude of striving hard to gain success but avoid a 'winning at all costs' attitude as this can lead to serious problems, like taking performance-enhancing drugs. Your able child is more precious as a person than just as a successful competitor in sport.

Provide a support service, as much as possible, including transport to training, trials and events. Taking away the hassle of organization frees up your child to concentrate upon the physical activity itself.

Be very careful about not allowing your able child to do too much during the formative years. A talented participator will always be in demand and there is a real danger of 'burnout'.

Know the difference between healthy encouragement and unhealthy pressure. The motivation to participate at an advanced level takes commitment, time and a single-mindedness of purpose. This motivation should be that of your able child. At tricky times, in particular, your able child will need encouragement to keep going, but the child should not compete unwillingly. Parents and carers need to avoid living vicariously through the talents of a child. Relentless driving is a very real danger and it can end in deep unhappiness and damaged relationships.

- Know when to involve a professional coach. Parents can help to a certain point but specialist knowledge is required. Tiger Woods' father, Earl, did a huge amount with his very young son but he recognized that he was not a PGA teaching professional. The advice in his wonderful book *Training a Tiger*, subtitled *The Official Book on How to be the Best*, is very sound.

  > *'Seeking professional help is not an indication of failure but rather an acknowledgement of what it takes to be successful. The next step is to see that you have taken your child as far as you can go on your own. Does this mean the end of your participation? No. It's just the next step in your child's development and should be a wonderful experience for both of you.' (p.169)*

  Although about golf, this book is a wonderful read for anybody with a talented child.

- Find quality time to give encouragement and support to your able child. The path to success is unlikely to be without difficulties and setbacks. It is at those most trying times that your child needs your patience, understanding and support.

- Try to get a variety of opportunities in different sports for your able child. There may be a potential talent of very high order waiting to be discovered. Many very able sportspeople are talented in more than one sport. Eventually a decision has to be taken, but it should be a decision based upon choice and knowledge.

- Work closely with your able child's school. It is through the school that many opportunities in the wider arena can be reached. A good relationship is highly desirable to accommodate training schedules. A young able swimmer, for instance, may need an early session at a full-size pool and this could have an effect on arrival time at school. Homework can be difficult at times of heavy commitment to competition.

- Make sure that your able child is given sufficient time to recover from an injury. A child who is a very important member of a team may be encouraged to play again too soon and a long-term problem can result. A caring watchful eye would be most beneficial.

- Take advantage of any masterclass coaching schemes or specialist facilities, such as a tennis centre, in your area. Working with other very able sportspeople gives a real challenge.

- Contact the Royal Academy of Dance, 36 Battersea Square, London SW11 3RA (telephone 020 7326 8000, email *info@rad.org.uk*, website *www.rad.org.uk*). Visit the website, in particular, to contact a registered teacher in your locality.

- Organize for your able child in dance to observe, work with and be taught by professional dancers and choreographers.

- Attend local and national performances by professional dance troupes.

- Keep your able child's future options open by maintaining other career possibilities. It is right to have ambition and to strive for success, but even promising children fail to make the grade or suffer a serious injury. Have a fallback position.

- See if local adult sports clubs have special facilities and opportunities for able children. Some schools co-operate with adult clubs to extend the range of possibilities.

- Build up a collection of suitable books for the designated sport. The 'Know the Game' series are produced in collaboration with national associations. They explain the rules clearly and have other helpful information. Many biographies are of interest but do not necessarily help with technique, but there are also books that aim to develop skills.

- Organize visits to games, competitions, tournaments and training sessions so that your able child can see top performers at work.

- Look at the availability of academic qualifications in physical education. A growing number of schools run an Advanced level in the subject and there is a section on physiology. Modern successful sportspeople take a great interest in diet and the theory behind optimum performance.

- Make contact with the governing body of the particular sport your able child is interested in. Visit the website *www.sportengland.org* and then go to the sport of major interest to you. Press 'Get Active' to go to an A–Z of sporting associations that give access to a wealth of advice and information.

# RELIGIOUS EDUCATION, PHILOSOPHY AND CITIZENSHIP

Some activities suggested here are for young children and they are indicated as such. Others are more suited for older children who have greater life experience and the maturity to handle complex issues.

Find time to discuss values and beliefs with your able and talented child, for they are central to these areas. Part of the model of ability includes leadership, negotiating, caring and good interpersonal skills. These are important talents to both the children themselves and society generally. Make sure that your child appreciates that you place as much importance on these abilities as those in mathematics and other subjects.

Obtain a subject-specific dictionary in the appropriate area. Specialized vocabulary plays an important part. *The Questions Dictionary of Religious Education* by Dr Elizabeth Ashton enables junior and lower-secondary-age children to understand the meanings of many complex words and concepts that are used in the subject (to order, telephone 0121 666 7878, email *sales@quest.pub.co.uk*). Oxford Paperbacks publish concise dictionaries of *The Christian Church* (edited by E. A. Livingstone) *Philosophy* (currently out of print) and *Politics*.

Encourage your able and talented child to read a quality newspaper every day and to watch one of the main news programmes on television in the evening. However, be careful about what your young, able children see for they may be affected more deeply than their peers and do not possess an adult capacity to handle really unpleasant events.

- Have a look at the 'Religion in Evidence' catalogue produced by TTS, Nunn Brook Road, Huthwaite, Sutton-in-Ashfield, Nottinghamshire NG17 2HU (telephone 0800 318686, email *sales@tts-group.co.uk*, website *www.tts-group.co.uk*). There are puppets, books, templates, posters, maps, jigsaws, videos and artefacts. Religions covered are Buddhism, Christianity, Hinduism, Islam, Judaism and Sikhism.

- Make a collection of political cartoons and ask your able child to interpret them. If your child has artistic skills, get him or her to convert news headlines into cartoons. Stick figures will suffice so long as the meaning is conveyed.

- Purchase, or borrow from the library, a copy of *The Philosophy Files* by Stephen Law. This is a collection of philosophical puzzles 'as old as the hills and as topical as today': Should I eat meat? How do I know the world isn't virtual? Where am I? What's real? Can I jump in the same river twice? Where do right and wrong come from? What is the mind? Does God exist? The fascinating text, that includes aliens, disembodied brains, virtual reality and even a talking pig, is enhanced by the entertaining illustrations of Daniel Postgate.

- Take a fresh look at Aesop's fables; there are many publications available. The Wordsworth Classics' version, *Fables*, illustrated by Arthur Rackham, has a good collection. Ask your able child to link chosen fables with contemporary events. Using a specific story to understand a general meaning that is then transferred to a new event is a good example of higher-order thinking and working at a second level of meaning beyond the literal.

- Obtain a copy of *Cat Song* by Andrew Matthews and Allan Curless. This beautiful picture book is an entrancing story of how God, having created cats with his singing, has to then 'discover' what cats can do. Ask your able child to write his or her own creation story, based upon the same principles, but for a different creature.

- Organize visits to meetings and events that are key elements in public life, for appropriately aged children – the magistrates' court, the Crown Court, council meetings, public debates, inquiry hearings, the Houses of Parliament, places of worship, festivals and so on.

- Buy copies of various newspapers on the same day. Ask your able child to look at the treatment of important political events, to spot the different approaches and to explain why the same event can be reported so differently.

- Encourage your able and talented child to play a more active role in public life, stressing the importance of participation for the health of a democratic society. Perhaps your able child could become a member of the School Council, be a committee member for a local organization, take part in a mock election, or hold a key post in a Young Enterprise company.

- Purchase, or borrow from the library, a copy of *Politically Correct Parables* by Robert Martin Walker. The author, an ordained Methodist minister from Texas, tells 15 cautionary tales, tongue-in-cheek, including 'The Geographically Dislocated Sheep' and 'The Alternatively

Committed Guests'. Let your child enjoy the humour. Ask your able child to write a story that illustrates the meaning of a parable. This, again, is working at a secondary, higher level than just literal meaning.

- Hold a family competition with each member, including your able child, writing a poem that has a theme from the areas of religious education, philosophy, politics or citizenship.

- Take advantage of relevant programmes on the television and radio. BBC1 has a weekly feature *The Politics Show* with both national and regional features. The same channel has the long-running *Question Time* with contrasting views on topical events and *This Week*, a political review. Individual programmes examine moral and social issues, including problems in developing countries. Within the BBC Learning Zone broadcasts on BBC2 there are appropriate but changing programmes. At the time of writing, there are *Rousseau in Africa: Democracy in the Making, What is Religion?* and *Looking for Hinduism in Calcutta*. Radio 4 also has much to offer: *Week in Westminster, Any Questions?, Any Answers?, The Westminster Hour* and *Today in Parliament*, to name a few.

- Select suitable letters to problem pages, ignoring those of a personal or romantic nature but, rather, concentrating upon those of a moral or social nature. Discuss with your able child the contrasting views that could be taken about the situation, recognizing that most real-life scenarios are not clear-cut. Knowing that an elderly person, with little money, is regularly involved in shoplifting, what could or should be done? What are the issues?

- Encourage your able and talented child to use his or her interpersonal skills by helping in the community, becoming a 'buddy' (friend) to a younger child at school, assisting at the local primary school or giving time to an established charity. For safety reasons, you may need to 'vet' the situation.

- Encourage reflection and higher-order thinking through the opportunities presented by the movement known as 'Philosophy for Children'. This stems from the work done by Matthew Lipman in the United States. He pioneered the work by involving children in philosophical thinking through considering situations within stories. Robert Fisher, a well-known educationalist in this country, has produced *First Stories for Thinking* that looks not only at the meaning of the stories but also considers key questions such as 'What is truth?', 'What is important about everyone?', 'Why are people different?' and 'What is a fair share?' There is also a very valuable introduction on principles and methods. A similar format for children aged 7–11 years is followed in Robert Fisher's *Stories for Thinking* with probing questions such as 'What do "want" and "need" mean?' and 'What do "knowing" and "believing" mean?' For older children, look for thought-provoking novels such as Malorie Blackman's brilliant *Noughts and Crosses* about prejudice and the bestseller *Sophie's World* by Jostein Gaarder, a mystery story that also forms an accessible introduction to philosophy and philosophers.

SAPERE is the Society for Philosophical Enquiry in Education (website *www.sapere.net*).

- Look for opportunities for your able child to meet others with similar ability and interests on enrichment courses run by LEAs or other organizations. Philosophy clubs and courses have been held in many areas including West Wales, Norfolk, West Sussex and Somerset.

- Use picture books, that are aimed at young children, on themes such as 'value', 'justice' and 'wisdom' for discussion by older children. A few suggestions to start: *The Monkey and the Panda* by Antonia Barber and Meilo So; *The Keeper of Wisdom* by Laura Berkeley and Alison Dexter; *The Huge Bag of Worries* by Virginia Ironside and Frank Rodgers; *Fly, Eagle, Fly!* by Christopher Gregorowski and Niki Daly; and *Dinosaurs and all that Rubbish* by Michael Foreman.

- Get your able child to write a 'Religious Tangled Tale', as used by the author on enrichment activities. The aim is to write a story that flows and makes sense and that includes religious education terms hidden in the story either as a correct spelling, such as commandments and prayer, or spelled differently such as arms (alms) and him (hymn) or as split words such as pass over (Passover).

- Ask your able, caring child to put together 'Twelve Truths' – a code by which people should live. This can have a religious base or a civics rationale or a combination of both. Discuss the reasons for the list that is compiled.

# SCIENCE

🔒 Find time to debate with your able and talented child issues concerning the moral and social implications of science, such as GM crops and cloning. This is an area of growing importance in the science curriculum.

🔒 Have a look at Michael Rosen's entertaining book *Centrally Heated Knickers*. It was commissioned by the STAR group (science, technology and reading), made up of the Royal Society of Chemistry, the Institute of Physics, Esso UK and the Design Council. It contains 100 poems about chemistry, physics, the environment, and design and technology. Ask your child to write poems on similar themes. Perhaps organize a family and friends competition.

🔒 Take advantage of the facilities provided by the Science Museum, Exhibition Road, London SW7 2DD (website *www.sciencemuseum.org.uk*). Make a visit to see their galleries, including the hands-on galleries for children. The IMAX cinema shows a changing programme of two-dimensional and three-dimensional films on a screen as high as five double-decker buses; for example, *Bugs* (three-dimensional) about a praying mantis and a tropical butterfly in the jungle of Borneo, *Ghosts of the Abyss* (three-dimensional) exploring the wreck of the *Titanic* and *Everest* (two-dimensional) following a team of international mountaineers (telephone 0870 870 4771). There are also special lecture demonstrations.

The Education Booking Office is 020 7942 4777 (email *edbookings@nmsi.ac.uk*). The number for general bookings and enquiries is 0870 870 4868. There is also a range of resources available.

🔒 Get your child to meet others of like mind and ability through enrichment sessions run by LEAs and the NAGC, summer schools and masterclasses at local universities.

📋 Make use of the opportunities in your home and garden. Get your child to observe life in the pond and the behaviour of various birds in the garden (which ones feed on a table, which on the ground, which on feeders, what their differing diets are, what their different patterns of behaviour are). Investigate the science behind routine tasks in the kitchen and elsewhere. *Riddles in Your Teacup* by Partha Ghose and Dipanker Home looks at ordinary everyday things that often contain surprises and puzzles when understood in terms of basic scientific principles. The message to children is 'Have fun thinking science!'. Also worth a look is Martin Gardner's *Entertaining Science Experiments with Everyday Objects*. The author shows how to re-create classic experiments with easily obtainable objects.

📋 Familiarize your child with the work of Russell Stannard. He was formerly Professor of Physics at the Open University. Russell Stannard remembers the excitement of discovering Einstein's theories for the first time and he is dedicated to passing this inspiration on to new generations. The Uncle Albert books – *The Time and Space of Uncle Albert, Black Holes and Uncle Albert* and *Uncle Albert and the Quantum Quest* – are designed for young readers to explore Einstein's theories through the action-packed adventures of famous scientist Uncle Albert and his intrepid niece Gedanken. *Ask Uncle Albert: 100$^{1}/_{2}$ Tricky Science Questions Answered* is rather different. Russell Stannard answers questions from Uncle Albert's postbag, sent in by children. The clear and direct answers are helped by illustrations. Russell Stannard's recent addition, *Dr Dyer's Academy*, is an entertaining and informative story. Jamie joins Dr Dyer's Academy only to discover that his science teacher hasn't a clue what she's talking about. The reader is challenged to see the truth behind popular scientific misconceptions. There is also a plot that engages with the moral responsibilities of science.

📋 Follow the Royal Institution Christmas lectures that are shown on television for five days over the Christmas period. Each year a presenter chooses a particular theme. There is an informative booklet to accompany the series.

📋 Play 'What If' in a scientific context. Get your child to speculate about questions such as 'What if it was light twenty-four hours a day?' and 'What if a mysterious illness wiped out the fox population of Britain?'. Get your able child to create other 'What If' questions.

📋 Have a look at the resources catalogue of the ASE (Association for Science Education), College Lane, Hatfield, Hertfordshire AL10 9AA (telephone 01707 283001, email *roboxley@ase.org.uk*, website *www.ase.org.uk*). Some publications are more obviously for teachers but there are many of more general interest. *Science is Like a Tub of Ice Cream – Cool and Fun* contains 100 poems from the ASE/Pfizer centenary competition and is beautifully illustrated in full colour with the children's own drawings. It is aimed at teachers, parents, carers and children. *Photo Opportunities: Science* is produced by Oxfam Publications in collaboration with the ASE. It has been designed to bring a global dimension to the delivery of primary science. *Science and Technology Ideas for the Under 8s* (ASE) has ten photocopiable units of fun ideas. *The Adventures of Charlie the Coulomb* by Brian Hodgson is a heavily illustrated story analogy to complement practical electrical circuit work at secondary science level.

🔢 Place your child at 'the frontier of knowledge'. Get him or her to consider a situation that has now been explored successfully but that your child does not know the 'answer' to. This allows ground-breaking thinking at a personal level.

🔢 Encourage the use and development of subject-specific vocabulary. Make available a science dictionary. Consider the purchase of *Signs and Symbols in Primary Science* compiled by Paul Burton and Lynne Wright, published by the ASE (contact details above). Oxford Paperbacks have more advanced concise dictionaries, including *A Concise Dictionary of Biology* edited by Elizabeth Martin, *The Concise Oxford Dictionary of Botany* edited by Michael Allaby, *A Concise Dictionary of Chemistry* edited by John Daintith, *The Concise Oxford Dictionary of Earth Sciences* edited by Ailsa Allaby, *The Concise Oxford Dictionary of Ecology* edited by Michael Allaby, *A Concise Dictionary of Physics* edited by Alan Isaacs, *The Concise Science Dictionary* edited by Elizabeth Martin and *The Concise Oxford Dictionary of Zoology* edited by Michael Allaby.

🔢 Consider subscribing to the magazine *New Scientist* (New Scientist Subscriptions, Freepost RCC2619, Haywards Heath, West Sussex RH16 3BR, telephone 08456 731731). All personal subscribers get free web access to the past ten years of *New Scientist* via the online archive. Alternatively, you can purchase copies from newsagents. There is a news update, strong articles and regular features. A particularly interesting item is 'The Last Word' where unusual questions are posed and experts write in with their responses. Examples include: 'Is it true that every time we take a breath of air or swallow a mouthful of water, we consume some of the atoms breathed or swallowed by Leonardo da Vinci?' and 'Can you explain in simple and commonsense terms why there is simultaneously a high tide on both sides of the Earth?' These are also collected in volumes and published by Oxford University Press.

🔢 Build up a collection of interesting books by 'popular' scientists, or borrow copies from a library. Richard Feynman, Steven Pinker, Ian Stewart, Stephen Hawking and Richard Dawkin are among authors to be considered for older children. Icon Books publish a series called Introducing. These are attractively illustrated and unusual guides. Examples include *Introducing Science* by Ziauddin Sardar and Borin Van Loon, which looks at the development of scientific studies, where science is taking us and trying to reconcile the advantages of science with the perils. *Introducing Chaos* by Ziauddin Sardar and Iwona Abrams gives an accessible introduction to an astonishing and controversial theory. Other titles to consider are *Introducing Time* by Ralph Edney, *Introducing Darwin and Evolution* by Jonathan Miller, *Introducing Einstein* by Joseph Schwartz and *Introducing Quantum Theory* by J. P. McEvoy.

🔢 Explore the possibilities within science fiction and fantasy. Many able children enjoy television programmes and books as long as there is a sustainable logic that is maintained. Having watched a programme like *The X-Files* or *Star Trek*, discuss with your able child the content and whether the basic ideas can be supported. There is now a new genre of book that speculates about the science behind literature and myths. *The Science of the Discworld*

links Professor of Mathematics Ian Stewart and reproductive biologist Jack Cohen with bestselling author Terry Pratchett. The book uses the magic of Discworld to illuminate the scientific rules that govern our world. The same authors have written *Science of Discworld II: The Globe* in which a Discworld novelette is woven together with cutting-edge scientific commentary on the evolution and development of the human mind, culture, language, art and science. Roger Highfield is a chemist, journalist and broadcaster. His *Can Reindeer Fly?* examines the science of Christmas considering questions such as 'What was the star of Bethlehem?' and 'How does Santa deliver all those presents in one night?'. He has more recently written *The Science of Harry Potter: How Magic Really Works.*

- Keep your eye on the television schedules. There are major series such as *The Life of Mammals* and Robert Winston's work such as *The Human Mind*, many regular natural history programmes, long-standing popular programmes such as *Horizon*, and features on animals and forensic science on the UK Horizons, Discovery and National Geographic channels. Garden series abound and one element is concerned with plant and soil science.

- Take a look at the specialist area of astronomy, if this is of interest to your able child. Consider acquiring a telescope or even a small astronomical observatory and subscribing to magazines such as *Astronomy Now*. Join SPA, the Society for Popular Astronomy, 36 Fairway, Keyworth, Nottingham NG12 5DU (website *www.popastro.com*). Visit a local observatory or major sites such as Jodrell Bank and the London Planetarium.

- Arrange family outings and visits to natural locations such as the seashore and to centres of scientific interest. Encourage a questioning approach with key words like 'how' and 'why'. Find out about places to visit in your own area or where you are on holiday, from libraries and tourist information centres. In Bristol, for instance, there are three main attractions (*www.at-bristol.org.uk*). Explore @ Bristol is an interactive science centre with four zones, special exhibitions and a planetarium. Wildwalk @ Bristol is a living rainforest in the heart of the city. Wildwalk takes you on a colourful journey through the variety of life on Earth using hundreds of live animals and plants, hands-on exhibits and stunning photography and film. IMAX theatre @ Bristol shows films on a giant four-storey screen in three-dimensional or two-dimensional formats.

  Alton Towers in Staffordshire is a fascinating place for children with its dramatic rides (telephone 01538 702200, website *www.altontowers.com*). The University of Manchester has collaborated with them to produce an education pack of resources, 'Science Alive', on potential energy, kinetic energy, forces, measuring speed and so on, for secondary-age pupils (able scientists of a younger age would be able to use them).

- Consider subscribing to *Focus*, the magazine of science and discovery (*www.focusmag.co.uk*). It has an interesting mixture of articles, photographs, news and investigations across a wide range of topics.

■ Get a copy of the catalogue of Tarquin Publications, Stradbroke, Diss, Norfolk IP21 5JP (website *www.tarquin-books.demon.co.uk*). They present science materials in a most attractive way, often in a model-making format. Some examples are *The Chemical Helix* by Gerald Jenkins and Magdalen Bear which explores the discovery and the explanation of the nature of the periodic table, first by making a model and then by using it to investigate why the chemical helix exists and why there are so many connections and relationships between elements. *Pivoting Parrots* by Anne Wild involves making some delightful card models while looking at the centre of gravity, balance and equilibrium. *The Puzzle of Symmetry Dice*, by Gordon Woods, leads to logical thinking about 34 special card dice and consideration of the curious effects in chemistry and biology of similar differences in the symmetries of molecules and living organisms.

■ Explore the possibilities of interpreting and drawing science cartoons. *Starting Points for Science* by Brenda Keogh and Stuart Naylor has some wonderful examples. It can be purchased through the ASE catalogue (contact details above). Get your able child to create some new cartoons that illustrate key ideas in science.

■ Encourage participation in school opportunities, such as science club activities after school, drop-in sessions at lunchtimes and the longer periods available in a Science Week.

■ Prompt thinking about science in picture books, stories and poems. A very direct example is *Mr Archimedes' Bath*, a picture book by Pamela Allen for young children. Once your child has taken a look, get him or her to create something similar on a different scientific principle. The ASE (contact details above) has in its catalogue 'Pencils, Poems and Princesses' which looks at how stories and poems can form the stimulus for a wide range of science and technology activities. The particular examples used are *Princess Smartypants* by Babette Cole, *Grandfather's Pencil and the Room of Stories* by Michael Foreman and the poetry book *Out and About* by Shirley Hughes. Once the idea is suggested, encourage your child to look for science in other books and poems.

■ Look for books that present science content in an unusual and interesting way. Nothing does this better than Jearl Walker's *The Flying Circus of Physics*.

■ Encourage your able child to join the youth section of organizations such as the RSPB (Royal Society for the Protection of Birds), conservation groups, wildlife trusts and local zoos.

■ Look at the activities organized by The British Association (for the advancement of science), Wellcome Wolfson Building, 165 Queen's Gate, London SW7 5HE (telephone 0870 770 7101, website *www.the-ba.net*). The Young People's Programme can be reached by telephone 020 7019 4943 or email *ypp@the-ba.net*. The British Association of Young Architects (BAYS) 'First Investigators' (5–8 year olds) and 'Young Investigators' (8–13 year olds) are schemes of children's science activities with silver and gold awards for the youngest children and bronze, silver and gold awards for 'Young Investigators'. Details are available by email from *bays@the-ba.net*. Members of the schemes receive *BAYSnews*

three times a year. BAYSdays are children's science festivals which are organized by the BA around the UK each year. They consist of 'workshops, dramas and lectures with lots of ideas to take away; hands-on activities where children "do" science guided by experts; a unique, exciting atmosphere created by a large number of enthusiastic visitors'. The whole approach can be summed up by this quote from the information pack: 'The BA aims to make science fun, accessible and relevant to all young people. BAYS members receive practical help in achieving this either in the home, in out of school clubs, through school/industry link groups or as part of the school curriculum.'

*CREST* (Creativity in Science and Technology) awards, via schools, are available at three levels – bronze, typically for ages 11–14, silver, typically for ages 14–16, and gold, typically for aged 16+. Check to see if your child's school or college is involved in the scheme. There are a number of sponsors, including AstraZeneca, who promote an 'Inspiring Science' programme (website *www.inspiringscience.co.uk*) which 'provides an opportunity for students to investigate and be inspired by science 24 hours a day, 7 days a week'.

Visit the Natural History Museum in London, either in person or online. A physical visit to the galleries and exhibitions provides a great experience. Find out what is available through the website (*www.nhm.ac.uk/education*). 'Investigate' is the museum's hands-on science centre for 7–14 year olds.

# TECHNOLOGY
## (FOOD, TEXTILES, DESIGN)

In the *New Scientist* magazine there is a special technology section. *New Scientist* can be purchased from newsagents or directly from New Scientist Subscriptions, Freepost RCC2619, Haywards Heath, West Sussex RH16 3BR (telephone 08456 731731).

Play to the higher-order thinking skill of evaluation. Ask your able and talented child to make judgements about features in the home and the man-made environment, clothing and other textile products. What are the main elements in the design? Are they effective? Could they be improved?

Organize family outings to locations that have strong design features. A popular visit for children is to Alton Towers, Alton, Staffordshire ST10 4DB (telephone 01538 702200, website *www.altontowers.com*). The University of Manchester has collaborated with them in the production of educational materials, including 'Design and Technology Alive' which has units on structures, mechanisms, control and design. They are aimed at secondary pupils but would be of interest to able children of a younger age.

Explore the resources catalogue of DATA (Design and Technology Association), 16 Wellesbourne House, Walton Road, Wellesbourne, Warwickshire CV35 9JB (telephone 01789 470007, email *DATA@data.org.uk*, website *www.data.org.uk*). As this is the recognized professional association in the subject area, many of the resources are aimed specifically at teachers. However, some materials will be of interest to parents and their children. Examples are *Inventing the 20th Century*, a book recounting the history of the most significant inventions of the twentieth century, 'Electronic Products' videos are available, which look at electronic control systems and their applications. While CAD and CAM videos, exploring Computer Aided Design and Computer Aided Manufacture, and a CD 'Food Manufacture – Behind the Scenes' take the secondary-age child, interactively,

through the product development stages. There is also a magazine for schools, called *Designing*, that is published termly and can be purchased by non-members. It provides inspiration and information for teachers and pupils across all phases, offering a lively mix of school projects, practical advice, topical features and display material.

- Encourage your able and talented child to build up a dictionary of terms used in technology. Purchase a copy of a technology dictionary. DATA (details above) publish an *Introduction to Design and Technology Vocabulary* for primary and lower-secondary pupils. Over 500 key words and definitions are included together with safety warnings to alert children and teachers to potential dangers.

- Ask if your able child's school is involved in the 'Taste of Success' Food Awards Scheme that is sponsored by J. Sainsbury. The scheme is aimed at encouraging children throughout the United Kingdom to enjoy learning about food. There are awards available at both primary and secondary school levels. There are online materials available on the Sainsbury's website at *www.j-sainsbury.co.uk/tasteofsuccess* or through links from the British Nutrition Foundation, website *www.nutrition.org.uk*

- Set problems, based upon the environment surrounding the family, for your able and talented child to try to solve in more ways than one. Redesign the school car park for maximum benefit. Imagine that a bridge is required to span a local stream or river. Find a more efficient way to store possessions in the child's bedroom.

- Encourage the concept of 'compromise'. Most completed schemes are not perfect but rather a balance between such considerations as cost, availability of materials, time allowed, life requirement and the impact socially, aesthetically and environmentally.

- Stress that the first solution may not be the best. Help your able child to develop a patient approach with regard to research, gathering data and attempting a variety of methods. Encourage him or her to generate more than one solution as the normal course of action.

- Look for opportunities to enable your child to work with others of similar ability and interests. This might occur through enrichment courses run by the LEA or other groups. Exchanging ideas and justifying proposals are important for development, especially as designers and technologists often work in teams. Improving communication skills and collaborative work are also important.

- See what the television schedules have to offer. Food programmes have proliferated. The *Young Chef of the Year* competition is a good opportunity to use evaluation skills. Does your child agree with the judges? Why or why not? *Ready, Steady, Cook* is a well-known format. Ask your child to plan and produce a meal from the ingredients described at the start of the programme. Use episodes of *Changing Rooms* for analysis and evaluation. Given what the owners said about their wishes, get your child to produce a suitable design. Ask your child to evaluate the work of the experts in terms

of what was asked. Design challenges, good food and garden changes feature strongly on the UK Bright Ideas channel. The UK Food channel has a feast of possibilities, including *Masterchef*. On terrestrial television, *Innovation Nation* was a series looking at new designs, which hopefully will be repeated, and *Seven Wonders of the Industrial World* has an accompanying book. The Discovery channel has a varied content but has relevance through programmes such as *Extreme Engineering*.

- Make time to discuss with your able child the ethical issues involved in technology – food additives, genetically modified food, antibiotics in animal growth, environmental costs and so on.

- Encourage your able child to be a discriminating and thoughtful consumer. Get him or her to put on 'technology glasses' in order to become informed users of products, natural and man-made, with reference to needs, purposes, financial and environmental costs.

- Do not lose sight of the practical skills. Design is important but so is making. Your child may be able in terms of 'working with tools, equipment, materials and components to make quality products' (a key element in the national curriculum programme). If your child has a particular interest, consider subscribing to magazines such as *Hobbies Handbook, Model Engineer, Engineering in Miniature, Practical Woodworking* or *Good Woodworking: The Big Book of Projects*. These are all reasonably priced and can be obtained from WH Smith and similar outlets, or on subscription direct from the publishers.

- Organize visits to exhibitions of the work of professional designers to appreciate the talents of those who lead the way. Also, take advantage of tours around manufacturing industry sites, cloth and clothing factories and food processing companies.

- Ask your able child to evaluate the quality of instructions for assembling items such as flat-packed furniture.

- Play to the 'oddball' sense of humour that is characteristic of many able children. Use some of the ideas in Edward de Bono's *Thinking Course for Juniors* (Direct Education Services Ltd, 35 Albert Street, Blandford Forum, Dorset) such as a method to stop a cat and a dog fighting, the design of a fun machine, a way of weighing an elephant and the design of a dog exercising machine. Make up some zany new problems or ask your child to suggest a problem and find solutions. It is the quality of the ideas that matter rather than the standard of the artwork in the drawings. Penguin have published two books of results by Edward de Bono – *Children Solve Problems* and *The Dog Exercising Machine*. Try to get a look at them.

- Take any opportunities for participation in 'Egg Races' where groups of children work in teams to solve specific problems.

- Encourage your child to communicate with companies so as to become involved in real projects.

- Try hard not to stifle your able child's curiosity. Clearly there are limits about interference with items in the home, for safety reasons as much as anything else, but 'idle, stupid thoughts' have often been the first steps towards a major development. Recognize that innovators break the normal boundaries.

- Have available, for younger children in particular, a big box of resources including paper, card, textiles, plastic, Lego, clay, plasticine, glue, scissors, string and so on for experimental and modelling purposes and to help assess the properties of materials.

- For those whose speciality is textiles, whatever the age, accumulate a collection of various materials, threads, wool, fabric paints and so on to facilitate creativity and experimentation.

- Try to keep a good balance between health and safety on the one hand and opportunity to experiment on the other. Clearly there are dangers that need guarding against, but being overprotective has serious problems too. These considerations are particularly important for younger children working with tools, sewing equipment and kitchen appliances. They will need supervision but not stifling.

- Explore the opportunities at your able child's school in terms of after-school club activities, enrichment events and 'open-door' time that is so essential for the completion of lengthy projects.

- Look for competitive events in your locality. Young Enterprise is a wonderful scheme for the post-16 age group.

- Get a copy of the extensive 'Active D&T' catalogue from TTS, Nunn Brook Road, Huthwaite, Sutton-in-Ashfield, Nottinghamshire NG17 2HU (telephone 0800 318686, email *sales@tts-group.co.uk*, website *www.tts-group.co.uk*). There is a wealth of material for constructing controllable vehicles, puppets, playgrounds and musical instruments. There are tools, wheels, balsa and wood packs, fabrics, threads, fastenings, mouldable materials, levers, gears and pulleys. Many of the materials could be used for projects from your able child's imagination as well as for prescribed tasks.

- Suggest that your able child looks at newspaper reports and television broadcasts on the latest fashion shows. Ask your child to make comments upon the suitability of the designs and the materials used.

# SECTION 3
## SOME RECOMMENDED CHILDREN'S FICTION

The books listed in the following pages are well known to the author, and are considered to be suitable for able and talented children for one or more of the following reasons. They:

- ☑ deal with an important issue
- ☑ are strong on word play and vocabulary extension
- ☑ display a particular sense of humour that fits many able children
- ☑ contain symbolism, second meanings, allegories, going beyond the literal
- ☑ involve magic, mystery, fantasy, intrigue
- ☑ display a mystical quality and strong sensitivity
- ☑ explore alternative ways of viewing the world
- ☑ present a way of exploring the reader's own emotions
- ☑ contain language that is haunting and beautiful
- ☑ have strong characters who are believable and not just caricatures
- ☑ involve complicated plots that demand concentration
- ☑ take a 'what if' approach
- ☑ present a challenge in terms of content and/or length
- ☑ stimulate the imagination strongly
- ☑ are very enjoyable!

The following cannot be anything approaching a definitive list. The recommended reading would fill the whole of this guide and then need some more space! Non-appearance in the list does not, therefore, mean that a book is not suitable for the able. It just may not have come to the attention of the author, or it could be the case that there is insufficient space. In any case, opinions differ. Look, therefore, for other recommendations by booksellers, commentators and Booktrust (details earlier).

On children's enrichment courses, the participants are often asked to bring a reading book with them or there is a short discussion about fiction. Clear patterns emerge even though there is a wide spread of interests. Able children, themselves, recommend titles to other children and to adults. This list has been influenced by that information.

The list has been set out in alphabetical order of author for ease of accesss. Age groups are mentioned in many areas but this has not been the method used for presentation. Some authors write for different age groups. Some readers defy their chronological age in terms of interest and capability. Do remember, however, the point made previously: coping with the mechanics of reading does not imply emotional maturity to understand feelings that only come with time. Picture books may seem to be aimed at young children, but many can be interpreted at a high level of thinking by older children.

## How to obtain the books

Note: This advice applies particularly to the children's fiction detailed below, but it also applies to texts described earlier in the book.

- The great majority of books recommended in this book are currently in print and they are available through the normal channels.

- They could be borrowed from a library. If the local library does not stock a particular book there is a system in place to contact larger book reserves in the area.

- A small number may be out of print but they are such good books that they are still recommended and worth tracing. There are a number of ways of setting about acquiring copies:

1. Second-hand books in general, including jumble sales and second-hand book shops.
2. Bargain book shops – they often stock remaindered books.
3. Websites such as *www.abebooks.co.uk* which states that it is the world's largest marketplace for second-hand and out-of-print books.
4. Individual booksellers, who often provide a tracing service, for example, *bookshopexmouth@btconnect.com*

# THE AUTHORS

## DOUGLAS ADAMS

*The Hitchhiker's Guide to the Galaxy* and its sequels are designed for an adult readership, but the zany sense of humour and oddball treatment have appealed strongly to able children who have a particular outlook on life.

## DAVID ALMOND

David Almond's books have a wonderful mystical quality. His debut novel *Skellig* was winner of the Carnegie Medal and the Whitbread Children's Book of the Year Award. It is a beautifully imaginative story that is unforgettable. *Kit's Wilderness* was the winner of the Silver Award in the Smarties 9–11 category, was shortlisted for the Guardian Prize and was Highly Commended for the Carnegie Medal. All David Almond's titles are worth strong consideration – *Heaven Eyes, Counting Stars, Secret Heart* and *The Fire-Eaters*.

## PHILIP ARDAGH

The Eddie Dickens trilogy is full of puns, jokes and hilarious nonsense. Word play features strongly. These books, and the more recent *Unlikely Exploits* trilogy, are ideal for those with a crazy sense of humour, especially boys.

## NINA BAWDEN

This popular and well-established author has many titles to her credit. She is excellent at describing feelings, some of them unpleasant. Particularly recommended are the classic *Carrie's War*, about a girl's extraordinary evacuation to Wales during the Second World War, and the more recent *Off the Road*, a futuristic tale that is a thought-provoking read, raising a raft of questions as to what the future holds and what is real quality of life. Meaty stuff!

## MALORIE BLACKMAN

She has a growing list for a wide age range. *Whizziwig*, a small, friendly alien is aimed at younger children. For upper juniors and lower-secondary-age children there are a number of adventures such as *Lie Detectives*. *Pig-heart Boy* is a powerful read, for perhaps 11+, concerning a controversial experiment to give a 13-year-old boy a transplant heart from a pig. *Noughts and Crosses* is an amazing book for teenagers about prejudice, injustice and racial division. Its unusual treatment only adds to the tension and the impact.

### 📖 QUENTIN BLAKE

He is not just the famous illustrator of the Roald Dahl books but a substantial author in his own right. His picture books are not only suitable for young children but also for older children to add a script at their own level of language and imagination. *Clown* is very good for predicting and converting the pictures into thoughts. Also look at *The Green Ship*, *The Story of the Dancing Frog* and *Cockatoos*. Anything he does has a stamp of quality.

### 📖 TIM BOWLER

Tim Bowler writes gripping stories with powerful content for perhaps 12+. *River Boy* was the winner of the Carnegie Medal in 1998. *Shadows* is particularly appropriate as it concerns a boy driven by his father to become a world squash champion. Also recommended is *Storm Catchers*. These books may be particularly suitable for boys.

### 📖 THERESA BRESLIN

There are many excellent books to consider, and for a variety of ages. The award-winning *Whispers in the Graveyard* mixes the ordinary with the extraordinary. For teenagers *Remembrance* is an epic novel about the First World War.

### 📖 RUTH BROWN

Among a number of brilliant picture books are *The World that Jack Built*, a thought-provoking book on the destruction of the environment, and the classic *A Dark Dark Tale* with its mystery and opportunity for prediction.

### 📖 ANTHONY BROWNE

With extraordinary illustrations, Anthony Browne's picture books have a character all of their own. *Voices in the Park* shows four different views of the same events. *Zoo* won the Kate Greenaway Award; it provokes consideration about animals.

### 📖 EION COLFER

The *Artemis Fowl* books are fast-moving, funny and brimming with creativity and imagination. There is an intoxicating mix of fairy myth and high technology. Perhaps for able readers from ten years upwards.

### 📖 SUSAN COOPER

The five books that make up The Dark is Rising series are now regarded as modern classics. They are wonderful fantasy stories set against ordinary life.

### 📖 GILLIAN CROSS

*The Demon Headmaster* series is very well known but there are more significant titles. *Wolf*, winner of the Carnegie Medal, is a powerful read. Highly acclaimed, *The Great Elephant Chase* won both the Smarties Prize and the Whitbread Award. *Pictures in the Dark* is intriguing and its symbolism is open to interpretation. *New World* is an indictment of the addictive nature of computer games.

## KEVIN CROSSLEY-HOLLAND

The author is fascinated by myths and traditional tales. For younger children his picture book (with Alan Marks) *The Green Children* is a beautiful re-telling of an old English folktale. His Arthurian trilogy *The Seeing Stone*, *At the Crossing Place* and *King of the Middle March* is brilliantly told through short, sharp chapters. Much period detail comes through. The books are well suited to able readers of ten years old or more.

## ROALD DAHL

Roald Dahl is a must with his inventiveness, fascinating characters and individual sense of humour. For younger children there are titles such as *The Enormous Crocodile* and *The Giraffe and the Pelly and Me*. Then come the delightful books like *Matilda* (with a love of books at its heart), *George's Marvellous Medicine* (a great introduction to the debate about GM foods), *The BFG* (with its wonderful word play) and a host of other characters – including Danny, Charlie, Fantastic Mr Fox and James. For teenagers three books of short stories with unusual twists are *The Great Automatic Grammatizator*, *The Wonderful World of Henry Sugar* and *Skin and Other Stories*.

## STEPHEN ELBOZ

Here is one of the answers to the much-asked question 'what shall I read after the Harry Potter books?' *A Handful of Magic*, *A Land without Magic* and *A Wild Kind of Magic* are full of mystery, excitement, invention and imagination. *The House of Rats* was the winner of the Smarties 9–11 Young Judges Prize. *Temmi and the Flying Bears* is a wonderfully written fantasy for junior-age children.

## ANN FINE

Look with confidence at the full range of titles as the author has won the Carnegie Medal twice, the Whitbread Children's Novel twice, the Guardian Children's Literature Award and the Smarties Prize. In addition, she has twice been voted Children's Writer of the Year and has been appointed Children's Laureate. For younger children there are titles including *The Chicken Gave It to Me*, *Bill's New Frock* and *How to Write Really Badly*. Moving up in age, look at *Bad Dreams* (the importance of being free to be yourself) and *Charm School* (condemning the idea that girls should simply be decorative). For older readers, there are many 'gems' including the dark tale *The Tulip Touch*, the prize-winning *Goggle-Eye* (the most unwanted boyfriend of them all), *Flour Babies* (an amazing story of adolescence and parenting), the absorbing *Step by Wicked Step* and the famous *Madame Doubtfire*.

## CORNELIA FUNKE

*The Thief Lord*, set in Venice, is an atmospheric thriller with a strong plot of twists and turns and engaging characters. *Inkheart* is a fascinating tale of stories that come to life.

## NEIL GAIMAN

One-time collaborator with Terry Pratchett, Neil Gaiman has produced a spellbinding story for older children in *Coraline*, that fascinates and frightens at the same time.

## 📖 ALAN GARNER

Although written many years ago, Alan Garner's fantasy stories rooted in folklore are still a great read. *The Weirdstone of Brisingamen* is a fast-moving and exciting tale and the mysterious *The Owl Service* won both the Guardian Award and the Carnegie Medal.

## 📖 ALAN GIBBONS

As well as a number of football stories, Alan Gibbons has written the Legendeer trilogy – *Shadow of the Minotaur, Vampyr Legion* and *Warriors of the Raven* – the first of which won the Blue Peter Book Award in the 'Book I Couldn't Put Down' category. The concept is an ingenious one – to put the action into a computer game that turns out to be all too menacingly real. They should appeal especially to boys from about ten years upwards.

Two powerful reads for older children are *The Edge*, a hard-hitting story involving both domestic and racist violence, and *Caught in the Crossfire*, a political novel, set in Britain, dealing with the aftermath of September 11th.

## 📖 MORRIS GLEITZMAN

Here is the male equivalent of Jacqueline Wilson in that Morris Gleitzman writes about sensitive subjects in a compelling, touching but funny manner. *Two Weeks with the Queen* deals with serious illness and other difficult material with a sure touch. *The Other Facts of Life* turns out not to be 'the birds and the bees' but starving people and the environment. *Second Childhood* is a thought-provoking book involving the main characters being reincarnations of famous people and the downsides of their actions.

## 📖 MARK HADDON

Very much for older children and adults, *The Curious Incident of the Dog in the Night-Time* is a stunningly original read telling Christopher's story in the first person. He is a 15 year old with Asperger's syndrome who is brilliant at maths and science but has terrible problems with human relationships. The book won the Guardian Children's Fiction Award and the Whitbread Award for Novel of the Year.

## 📖 LIAN HEARN

*Across the Nightingale Floor*, for older children and adults, deals with a titanic struggle in medieval Japan. It has beauty and mysticism as well as brutality. *Grass for His Pillow* is the sequel in this epic tale.

## 📖 NAT HENTOFF

*The Day They Came to Arrest the Book* is a thought-provoking novel about events when a small group of parents and students brand *Huckleberry Finn* as racist, sexist and immoral. This opens up, for teenagers, the world of censorship and political correctness.

## 📖 MARY HOFFMAN

Time-slip stories set in Italian cities and their counterparts provide rich reading, a strong plot and engaging characters in *Stravaganza: City of Masks* and *Stravaganza: City Of Stars*. Fantasy and imagination abound.

## 📖 ANTHONY HOROWITZ

*Groosham Grange* is a seriously weird school with hilarious goings-on. A strong sense of humour is also evident in the series involving Tim Diamond, probably the worst detective in the world, and his brother Nick. There are puns, jokes and take-offs galore. The titles are *The Falcon's Malteser*, *South by South East* and *Public Enemy Number Two*. For slightly older children, perhaps 12 years and upwards, are the Alex Rider books. He is a teenage James Bond who gets involved in tense, exciting adventures that should be particularly good for boys. Look out for *Stormbreaker, Point Blanc, Skeleton Key, Eagle Strike* and *Scorpia*.

## 📖 LESLEY HOWARTH

Her books tend to be unusual but very thought-provoking. Two titles, among many others, to consider are *Maphead*, winner of the Guardian Children's Fiction Award, and *Weather Eye*, looking at children's anxieties about the environment and climate change.

## 📖 EVA IBBOTSON

This is another author whom Harry Potter fans would likely enjoy. The books are highly imaginative and concern ghosts, wizards and witches. Particularly good is *The Secret of Platform 13*. The highly acclaimed *Journey to the River Sea* is different, being set in the exotic world of the Amazon. It won the Smarties Gold Award.

## 📖 BRIAN JACQUES

The 'Redwall' series of books of animal battles and adventures has proved tremendously popular, with boys in particular, in the junior and lower secondary-age range.

## 📖 ROBIN JARVIS

Robin Jarvis writes big, expansive stories with interesting settings and larger-than-life characters. They are lengthy but very exciting and are best suited, perhaps, to 11 year olds and upwards. Concentration brings reward with *The Deptford Histories* (trilogy), the three books that make up *The Deptford Mice*, the Whitby trilogy and the chilling *Tales From the Wyrd Museum* (three books).

## 📖 DIANA WYNNE JONES

Diana Wynne Jones is a prolific writer of brilliant fantasy stories. Fans of Harry Potter should love her wizard, Chrestomanci, who features in a series of imaginative and inventive books. *Charmed Life* won the 1977 Guardian Award for Children's Books and introduces the worlds of Chrestomanci. There are many other books, including the acclaimed *The Merlin Conspiracy*.

## 📖 NORMAN JUSTER

A modern classic, *The Phantom Tollbooth* has fabulous word play, and symbolism and messages abound. Wit and humour, of a very special kind, are central to the book. Milo visits the most incredible places – The Doldrums, Dictionopolis, Digitopolis, Illusions, Reality and many others. The book is also packed with extraordinary characters.

## 📖 JUDITH KERR

*When Hitler Stole Pink Rabbit* is a powerful story about prejudice. It has two sequels, *The Other Way Round* and *A Small Person Far Away*.

## 📖 CLIVE KING

A modern classic about friendship, *Stig of the Dump* tells the story of Barney who says he has discovered a boy living wild in the dump.

## 📖 DICK KING-SMITH

There are many titles, some for young children, others for a little bit older. The majority concern animals. They are charming and entertaining but some are more than that.

*Saddlebottom* is very much about prejudice and being different. *The Hodgeheg* contains delightful word play. *Harriet's Hare*, the winner of the 1995 Children's Book Award, is full of magic, sensitivity and mysticism. There is a wonderful plot in *The Fox Busters* but there is also a strong element of word play.

*The Roundhill* is very different. It involves the revisiting of a favourite place by the ghost of Alice Liddell. The book deals with rites of passage, the passage of time and the handing down of valued experiences from generation to generation. Then, of course, there is the unforgettable *The Sheep-Pig*, winner of the Guardian Award. Do not ignore either two books for older children that have a more serious feel – *The Crowstarver* and *Godhanger*.

## 📖 C. S. LEWIS

The seven books about the land of Narnia still read tremendously well. They are excellent fantasy stories. There is also a great deal of second-level meaning and symbolism, especially in *The Lion, the Witch and the Wardrobe*.

## 📖 JOAN LINGARD

There are a number of titles for younger children, but it is the writing for those who are older that is better known. The Kevin and Sadie stories deal with religious conflict in Belfast and then hardship in London. *The Guilty Party* is a very topical novel about a teenager drawn into conflict with politics and the law. *Natasha's Will* has a strong historical flavour, starting with the Russian Revolution and the First World War.

## 📖 MICHELLE MAGORIAN

Winner of the Guardian Children's Fiction Award, *Goodnight Mister Tom* is an emotional story involving the evacuation of Willie Beech at the start of the Second World War. Also for a middle age range, in *A Spoonful of Jam* Elsie fights against bullying and avoids a gang by accepting a part in a play at the local theatre.

## 📖 MARGARET MAHY

Margaret Mahy has many books to her credit across a wide range of ages. She has twice won the Carnegie Medal, first for *The Haunting*, a psychological thriller with ghosts and strange happenings, and then for *The Changeover*, a supernatural thriller for teenagers.

Her versatility is shown with the picture story book *A Busy Day for a Good Grandmother*, the hilarious *A Villain's Night Out* for a middle age, *Memory*, winner of the Young Observer Teenage Fiction Award and *Twenty-four Hours*, an emotional rollercoaster for young adults.

## 📖 JAN MARK

Here is another author who writes across the age range. Young readers will be delighted with titles like *My Frog and I*. Jan Mark has won both the Penguin/*Guardian* competition and the Carnegie Medal for *Thunder and Lightnings*, a book about aeroplanes and friendship. *The Sighting* suits older readers and *Heathrow Nights* is considered particularly good for adolescent boys.

## 📖 GERALDINE McCAUGHEREAN

Geraldine McCaugherean has a wide repertoire. Young children are catered for with titles like *Wizziwig and the Singing Car*, but titles for older readers are better known. *Forever X* has as its centre the hotel where every day is Christmas Day. There are thought-provoking ideas on relationships, parenting and the nature of childhood. The witty *A Pack of Lies: 12 Stories in One*, won the Guardian Children's Fiction Award and the Carnegie Medal. *The Stones are Hatching* is a strong read based upon myths and legends.

## 📖 MICHAEL MORPURGO

Here is an outstanding writer, who is lyrical and appealing to the emotions. The books are often quite short. *Billy the Kid* mixes football, the Second World War and the memories of an 80-year-old man. The book is moving and charming but it is never over sentimental. Some grim events are covered. *Kensuke's Kingdom* is an amazing story about a boy's voyage of discovery of himself and the world. *The Wreck of the Zanzibar* deals with community life in the Scillies. Two evacuees and their encounter with two German fliers are at the heart of *Friend or Foe*. There are so many others with compassionate writing interwoven with issues. A wide age range is catered for and boys would find much to interest them.

## 📖 WILLIAM NICHOLSON

His Wind on Fire trilogy is highly acclaimed. The three books – *The Wind Singer*, *Slaves of the Mastery* and *Firesong* are imaginative, full of action and compelling reading. They are all set in an imaginary kingdom.

## 📖 JENNY NIMMO

*The Snow Spider*, the first book of the trilogy of the same name, won the Smarties Grand Prix Award. The other two books are *Emlyn's Moon* and *The Chestnut Soldier*. For perhaps the able 8–12-year-old range. They interweave magic and folklore. *The Rinaldi Ring* is a story of love, hate and loss coming out of the destruction of the First World War.

## 📖 ANDREW NORRISS

Winner of the Whitbread Children's Book of the Year, *Aquila* is a story of hope – if you really want to do something then find the right vehicle and use all your determination – and contains powerful imagery. *Bernard's Watch*, an exploration of time, has a strong plot, interesting characters, intrigue and imagination.

## 📖 PHILIPPA PEARCE

Philippa Pearce is the author of a number of outstanding books that are regarded as classics. Carnegie Medal winner *Tom's Midnight Garden* is a magical, mystical book that leaves space for a number of interpretations. *The Battle of Bubble and Squeak* won the Whitbread Award and there are other memorable books including *A Dog So Small* and *Minnow on the Say*.

## 📖 ANN PILLING

The Guardian Children's Fiction winner, *Henry's Leg* is a deceptively simple story. There is an engaging combination of wit, adventure, humour and sadness, and there is no easy happy-ever-after ending. *The Empty Frame* provides a web of mystery and murder.

## 📖 POETRY

Many able children appreciate the qualities of good poetry with its need to express ideas in limited space. However, tastes vary considerably. One suggestion is to take a look at an anthology such as *The Nation's Favourite Children's Poems* published by the BBC. It contains a wide variety of poets and themes. For those who have a particular sense of humour, try *The Penguin Book of Nonsense Verse* selected and illustrated by Quentin Blake. Benjamin Zephaniah's *Talking Turkeys* and *Funky Chickens* are highly valued for their rhythms and real-life poems that deal with issues in an imaginative way. *Please Mrs Butler* by Allan Ahlberg is a collection of poems about school. Michael Rosen has a number of collections that are popular with children. Roger McGough tries to make his poems accessible. For older children a way to find out what you like is to read the poems that are printed in newspapers such as the *Guardian* on a weekly basis.

## 📖 TERRY PRATCHETT

Terry Pratchett is immensely popular with many able children. His eccentric humour strikes a chord. The Johnny Maxwell series is particularly ideal for boys. *Only You Can Save Mankind* is a thought-provoking challenge to shooting down aliens in computer games. *Johnny and the Bomb* has brilliant time switches. The comparisons between the Second World War and the 1990s are devastating. You actually question what advances in society have really meant. In *Johnny and the Dead* Terry Pratchett makes sharp and pointed comments upon human nature, religion, greed and so-called progress. All three books are very funny indeed. The Nomes trilogy – *Truckers*, *Diggers* and *Wings* – are full of invention, wit and humour. *The Amazing Maurice and His Educated Rodents* is a brilliant book that deservedly won the Carnegie Award. A streetwise tomcat, a stupid boy who plays a pipe and a band of rats with odd names, provide an incredible story of humour, darkness, power, enjoyment and mystery that also deals with the issue of getting on with those you do not like. The extensive Discworld series for adults has many fans among the ranks of able children who love the offbeat humour and incredible characters.

## 📖 SALLY PRUE

*Cold Tom* is a magical, mystical story for children of, perhaps, 11+ years old, about relationships and belonging. There is an imaginative and unusual style. The book was the winner of the Branford Boase Award and the Nestlé Smarties Silver Award. *The Devil's Toenail* is a thoughtful story about a bullied boy and his coming to terms with the problems. *Ryland's Footsteps* concerns the relationship of a boy with his father among some fascinating ingredients including a lizard that burns, a secret cave and a prisoner's daughter.

## 📖 PHILIP PULLMAN

Many people regard Philip Pullman as the greatest modern writer of children's fiction. He is an amazing author with a wide range of material. There are magical, enchanting stories for younger children. *Clockwork* has the potent combination of brilliant ideas, powerful storyline, mystery, morality and joy. The context of clocks, time and mechanisms is itself highly enjoyable. *The Firework-Maker's Daughter*, winner of the Smarties Book Prize, has a haunting beauty in the messages conveyed about care, love and wisdom, and how they combine together to produce a very special dignity. The adventures *Spring-Heeled Jack* and *Count Karlstein* use a mixture of words and cartoons (*Count Karlstein* is now available in a fuller text version). For slightly older children comes *I Was a Rat!*, a clever, witty and inventive variation on the Cinderella story. *The New Cut Gang* stories, set in Victorian London, are more straightforward. For older children there is also a Victorian setting for the Sally Lockhart series – *The Ruby in the Smoke*, *The Shadow in the North*, *The Tiger in the Well* and *The Tin Princess*. They are action-packed adventure thrillers. For teenagers there are *The Broken Bridge*, an identity-crisis novel, and a tragic thriller, *The Butterfly Tattoo*.

Saving the best for last, the trilogy His Dark Materials is an extraordinary piece of writing. *Northern Lights* is a strong fantasy adventure that sets up the sequels, *The Subtle Knife* and *The Amber Spyglass*. It won the Carnegie Medal and the Guardian Children's Fiction Award. The amazing characters, including armoured polar bears, witches, spectres and harpies, are matched by three incredible artefacts, the alethiometer, the subtle knife and the amber spyglass. The reader is drawn into a demanding discussion about good and evil, original sin, religion and the enigmatic 'dust'. So good is the third book, *The Amber Spyglass*, that it was awarded the Whitbread overall award, the first time that a children's book has been so judged. The full impact of the trilogy can be felt only by older children.

### 📖 PHILIP REEVE

In *Mortal Engines*, Philip Reeve has written an exciting, highly entertaining, adventure story. This is an inventive, original book as London moves across the world on wheels, capturing and eating smaller towns and cities. The gripping story has been continued in *Predator's Gold*.

### 📖 MORTON RHUE

For older children, *The Wave* is a terrifying tale of a classroom experiment going badly wrong. It has strong political messages.

### 📖 J. K. ROWLING

The Harry Potter books need no introduction and they have been a publishing sensation. They clearly must be included for their fantasy, magic, inventiveness and absorbing storylines. The greatest tribute to the author is that she has made reading 'cool'. She has generated amazing excitement. One point to be made is that, especially as Harry grows up and the atmosphere grows even darker, the later books are not aimed at young children.

### 📖 LOUIS SACHAR

*Holes* is a brilliant, powerful book where Louis Sachar uses a no-nonsense, very direct style. A strong plot is delivered with pace as three distinct strands are woven together. Stanley Yelnats has to survive life in a brutal juvenile centre to which he has been sent through a miscarriage of justice. There is much meat for able readers and boys, in particular, will be engaged.

## 📖 JON SCIESZKA AND LANE SMITH

Do not miss the brilliantly funny picture books of this highly successful pair. *The True Story of the 3 Little Pigs* tells a traditional story from the wolf's perspective. *The Maths Curse* is a brilliant conception, mixing mathematics and fun. *Baloney* is based upon wonderful word play. *Squids will be Squids* tells modern fables in an hilarious manner.

## 📖 NICKY SINGER

Winner of the Blue Peter Book of the Year, *Feather Boy* is a wonderful book about bullying: a mystery, with convincing school scenes, and full of second meanings and symbolism. 'You can do it. You can fly' is the motto of a story that lives long in the memory.

## 📖 LEMONY SNICKET

A Series of Unfortunate Events, starting with *The Bad Beginning*, is an unusual set of books in which the author advises potential readers to go elsewhere! One feature is that there are no happy endings. Another marked element is the brilliantly funny word play that has a strong appeal to many able children. Even the titles are carefully chosen such as *The Miserable Mill*, *The Vile Village* and *The Hostile Hospital*.

## 📖 PAUL STEWART (and CHRIS RIDDELL)

Paul Stewart has some gripping stories to just his name – *The Midnight Hand* and *The Wakening*. They are pacy and creepy. However, his most famous titles are those produced in collaboration with Chris Riddell. The Edge Chronicles starts with *Beyond the Deepwoods* and continues with *Stormchaser, Midnight over Sanctaphrax, The Curse of the Gloamglozer, The Last of the Sky Pirates* and *Vox*. They are very popular with able children. The Edgeworld is a fantastic world teeming with incredible characters. The books are fast-moving adventure stories with amazing flora and fauna influencing the action. The joint authors are also responsible for a spoof Tolkien novel called *Muddle Earth* and picture books for young children, *Rabbit's Wish* and *The Birthday Presents*, looking at kindness and friendship.

## 📖 ROBERT SWINDELLS

The author has a large number of titles including the uncompromising *Stone Cold*, winner of the Carnegie Medal. They are powerful stories, many for older readers, which deal with issues. *Wrecked* looks at under-age drinking. *Abomination* has religious intolerance as its theme. Bullying and extortion are dealt with in *Dosh*. *Unbeliever* concerns a religious sect. Prejudice plays a large part in *Invisible!*. There are also sinister tales like *Nightmare Stairs* for the middle age range.

## 📖 G. P. TAYLOR

*Shadowmancer* was an unexpected big seller. There is a fascinating mixture of smuggling and greed in Whitby with a fantasy element and a titanic battle between good and evil. His second novel, *Wormwood*, has also attracted much favourable attention.

## 📖 COLIN THOMPSON

Colin Thompson creates the most incredible picture books that are very special indeed. They are packed with detail and combine stunning visual images with important messages and truths. *The Tower to the Sun* foretells of a world destroyed by pollution and clutter.

*The Last Alchemist* debates the nature of true wealth. *How to Live Forever* concerns a missing book that has the secret of everlasting life but the story emphasizes that to live forever is not to live at all. In *The Paradise Garden* Peter learns not just to escape but to create peace and contentment around him. All ages can take pleasure from the extraordinary illustrations in these truly amazing books.

## ROBERT WESTALL

There is a huge selection to choose from by this prolific author. Winner of the Carnegie Medal, *The Scarecrows* is a tense and dramatic story with plenty of opportunity for interpretation. *Falling into Glory* is a powerful read for teenagers, pulling no punches about a very sensitive subject, a love affair between a young man and one of his teachers. *Blitzcat*, winner of the Smarties Prize, uses Lord Gort, a cat, to describe linked episodes in the Second World War. Among many other titles, *The Kingdom by the Sea* won the Guardian Children's Fiction Award and *The Machine Gunners* was awarded the Carnegie Medal.

## JACQUELINE WILSON

Girls, in particular, devour everything and anything written by the extraordinary Jacqueline Wilson, and no wonder. She has the brilliant knack of being able to write about difficult issues but with sensitivity and humour. It is a wonderful gift. Every book she has written is worth reading. *Vicky Angel* tackles bereavement and guilt. The loss of a loved one is also at the heart of *The Cat Mummy*. *Video Rose* shows the dangers of being able to see into the future. A powerful read is in store with *The Illustrated Mum* in which Dolphin and Star have to deal with the mental illness of their mother Marigold. *The Story of Tracy Beaker* is very moving, giving wonderful insight into the world of children in institutions who desperately want to be loved but who sometimes do not help themselves. There are also books for younger readers like *Lizzie Zipmouth* and *The Werepuppy*. For older children there is the series *Girls in Love*, *Girls Under Pressure* and *Girls Out Late*. One could go on and on about this multi-award winning author.

Sincere apologies for the many wonderful authors and books not included in this annotated list that has to be of limited length.

# A selection of titles from Network Educational Press

## ABLE AND TALENTED CHILDREN COLLECTION

*Effective Provision for Able and Talented Children* by Barry Teare
*Effective Resources for Able and Talented Children* by Barry Teare
*More Effective Resources for Able and Talented Children* by Barry Teare
*Challenging Resources for Able and Talented Children* by Barry Teare
*Enrichment Activities for Able and Talented Children* by Barry Teare

## ACCELERATED LEARNING SERIES

*Accelerated Learning: A User's Guide* by Alistair Smith, Mark Lovatt & Derek Wise
*Accelerated Learning in the Classroom* by Alistair Smith
*Accelerated Learning in Practice* by Alistair Smith
*The ALPS Approach: Accelerated Learning in Primary Schools* by Alistair Smith & Nicola Call
*MapWise* by Oliver Caviglioli & Ian Harris
*The ALPS Approach Resource Book* by Alistair Smith & Nicola Call
*Creating an Accelerated Learning School* by Mark Lovatt & Derek Wise
*ALPS StoryMaker* by Stephen Bowkett
*Thinking for Learning* by Mel Rockett & Simon Percival
*Reaching out to all learners* by Cheshire LEA
*Leading Learning* by Alistair Smith
*Bright Sparks* by Alistair Smith
*Move It* by Alistair Smith

## OTHER TITLES

*Help Your Child to Succeed: The essential guide for parents* by Bill Lucas & Alistair Smith
*Help Your Child to Succeed: Toolkit* by Bill Lucas & Alistair Smith
*The Thinking Child* by Nicola Call with Sally Featherstone
*The Thinking Child Resource Book* by Nicola Call with Sally Featherstone
*Becoming Emotionally Intelligent* by Catherine Corrie
*That's Science!* by Tim Harding
*That's Maths!* by Tim Harding
*Foundations of Literacy* by Sue Palmer & Ros Bayley
*With Drama in Mind* by Patrice Baldwin
*Effective Learning Activities* by Chris Dickinson
*Lessons are for Learning* by Mike Hughes
*Raising Boys' Achievement* by Jon Pickering
*Best behaviour* and *Best behaviour FIRST AID* by Peter Relf, Rod Hirst, Jan Richardson & Georgina Youdell
*Closing the Learning Gap* by Mike Hughes
*Leading the Learning School* by Colin Weatherley
*Strategies for Closing the Learning Gap* by Mike Hughes & Andy Vass
*Effective Teachers* by Tony Swainston
*Effective Teachers in Primary Schools* by Tony Swainston
*Transforming Teaching and Learning* by Colin Weatherley, Bruce Bonney, John Kerr & Jo Morrison
*Thinking Skills & Eye Q* by Oliver Caviglioli, Ian Harris & Bill Tindall
*Think it–Map it!* by Oliver Caviglioli & Ian Harris
*Reaching out to all thinkers* by Ian Harris & Oliver Caviglioli

For more information and ordering details, please consult our website www.networkpress.co.uk